Yes You Can

YES YOU CAN

A Political Insider's Guide to
Winning Your Campaign

Gunnar G. Hardy

Hatty Hardy Publishing

Copyright © 2017 by Gunnar G. Hardy
All rights reserved. No part of this publication may be reproduced, distributed, or transmitted in any form or by any means, including photocopying, recording, or other electronic or mechanical methods, without the prior written permission of the publisher, except in the case of brief quotations embodied in critical reviews and certain other noncommercial uses permitted by US copyright law.

For permission requests, write to the publisher, addressed "Attention: Permissions Coordinator," at the address below.

Hatty-Hardy Publishing
412 N. Main St. Suite 100
Buffalo, WY, 82834
www.yycbook.co.uk

Printed in the United States by CreateSpace, an Amazon.com Company

First Edition: December 2017

10 9 8 7 6 5 4 3 2 1

ISBN 978-1979247344

Library of Congress Control Number: 2017919622

"To my loving mother for always encouraging me to be the best that I can be."

CONTENTS

Introduction x

Section One : The Campaign Starts With YOU! .. 1

Step To Success One 2
Be Confident In What You Stand For

Step To Success Two 34
Do Some Research

Section Two : Getting Ready To Run 55

Step To Success Three 56
Make A Budget

Step To Success Four 69
Fundraising

Section Three : Surrounding Yourself With Winners 87

Step To Success Five 88
Find Your Political Partner

Step To Success Six 94
Building A Successful Team

Section Four : Planning And Winning 121

Step To Success Seven 122
Make A Plan

Step To Success Eight 130
Get Out There!

In Conclusion 142

INTRODUCTION

Putting yourself up for election is not only difficult but downright terrifying. Believe me, I would know. When I first ran for election I absolutely had no idea what to do, where to turn or who to trust, I honestly wished someone could have guided me through the complicated network of minefields we call modern politics. Over the years, my skills grew, and the roadblocks to success started to fade away, then I asked myself if there was a way that I could help others who wanted to make lasting change and come out on top. This book provides just that.

Hands-on strategies you can implement easily, no matter your experience in the political arena. From discovering yourself and your passion, to making savvy political decisions. Building a great campaign team to solid campaign budgeting. Whether you need an excellent strategy to beat your opposition, or want to learn how to use your opposition to your advantage. Discover what it takes to be an exceptional candidate and a winning politician in this book. Yes, YOU Can!

-Gunnar

Yes You Can

SECTION ONE
The Campaign Starts With YOU!

STEP TO SUCCESS ONE

Be Confident in What You Stand For

Successful people have fear, successful people have doubts, and successful people have worries. They just don't let these feelings stop them.

– T. Harv Eker

Running for a public office or just want to thrive in political campaigning? The first step in achieving this lofty goal is to be confident in your beliefs and what you stand for.

Essentially, confidence is the firm belief that you are both capable and worthy of doing or achieving something. Confidence also deals with the ability to appreciate and value yourself. By the time you appreciate yourself, you will soon realise that confidence follows almost immediately. Now, let's get started on your journey!

Who am I? Am I good enough? Am I worthy?

These attitudes deny people the right to choose the opportunity of taking on an exciting adventure in their lives, applying for a job they'd be a perfect fit for and even running for office. In short, learning how to build personal confidence at any age, is pivotal for a happier, healthier, and more productive life.

The following are top tips to becoming the confident politician you want to be. These tips will help you function in a more efficient way and help you eliminate any potential hinderance to your optimal performance.

Reduce To-dos

Amazingly, it has been found that a "To Do" list does not increase your productivity, rather it can hamper it. Instead of serving as a soft reminder, it can be an unnerving source of unnecessary pressure. A lot of people feel anxious when looking at their list partway to completion.

This "personal" failure often either motivates an individual to attempt to finish everything quickly with subpar results or give up on their list altogether; neither of which will bring you happiness.

This comes down to the fact that people make the wrong kind of list: if you pen down everything you want to do in one go, you'd start feeling trapped. Instead, pen down two things you really want to get done before the end of your day and focus on these two only. Don't write down two colossal projects. Rather, pen one big goal and one small. If you do this daily, you'll realise that within a month all your projects will begin to fall into a healthy rhythm.

Build your self-image

Try to see yourself in a different light: list all the things you dislike about yourself and challenge yourself to see what the opposite would look like in your life; this way, you can pave a path to turn your dislikes around. If you dislike aspects of your character, try not to change them immediately, rather, redirect them. If you feel as if you are too aggressive, try channelling your aggression toward other ventures like joining a gym and working out. Here, you'll also learn how to calm down when you feel a bout of rage coming on. If you feel you are too direct, channel this to a good cause; standing up to a boss, or setting up your own company. You'll learn to be direct but polite.

If what you dislike about yourself has to do with aspects of your body, it's a harder task but not impossible to surmount. Of course, you can tone yourself in the gym, but this takes time. Learning to love your yourself is fundamental.

Learning

Nothing will give you a more positive feeling about yourself than learning something new. And now this is easier than ever. There are loads of free highly accredited classes that can be accessed online that you could take on to learn a new skill.

Fake it till you make it

Confidence builds confidence: even when you don't feel confident, act as if you are. If you feel frightened or in doubt, think, "What would the confident me do?" and then do it. If you keep acting as if you already are the positive version of you, you would find yourself being the positive/motivated version of You.

Joy

Take a look at your life, the people, the things you collected, and met: does it bring you joy? How do you feel after meeting a person? Happy? Great! Energised? Great! Drained? Wrong! Deflated? Wrong! If you feel low, exhausted or upset after meeting or talking to someone, cut them from your life. Always rememeber that no one has the right to make you feel that way. The same goes for the items around you: do they remind you of good things? If not, redecorate a bit or tidy up. You could even reshape some items to save money. It'll help generate a positive vibe around you.

You're scared to go somewhere because you feel you're not up to it, will be laughed at or will stick out? Are you sure about that? What if you've just talked yourself out of the best thing that could happen to you? Think "what the hell?" and just do it anyway.

STOP!

If your insecurities sneak up on you, stop them dead in their tracks. Think or say "STOP IT!" aloud, and try to refocus on something stupid. Whenever you start thinking badly about yourself or something you want to do, train your brain into thinking up the lyrics of a weird children's song and very soon you'll be distracted.

Find your inner "Lion"

If all of these fail, roar! If you find yourself low on confidence,stand in front of the mirror and start picturing yourself as a lion - strong, powerful and king or queen of the jungle. Imagine yourself growing stronger and more confident, then ROAR!! The gush of energy this releases will leave you feeling energised and strong.

Know What You Are Good At

"Knowing yourself is the beginning of all wisdom."

—Aristotle

To truly know yourself is the most crucial skill, you can ever possess. When you know who you truly are, you know what you need to do, instead of seeking the permission of others to do what you already know you ought to do. It allows you to go around a myriad of frustration caused by investing time in the wrong things. Yes, life is supposed to be full of trial and error, but this helps you find the best areas for you to experiment in the first place. Once you know yourself, you will have more confidence, understand your purpose, and begin making a bigger impact on the world.

So how can you know who you genuinely are and what you ought to do in life? Here are the steps you need to take in order to know your true self:

1. Be quiet.

You cannot know yourself until you take the time to be still and reflect inwardly. Many people don't know themselves because the smallest of silence scares them; it feels too uncomfortable to be alone with every flaw staring back at them. But it isn't until you get alone, evaluate yourself and are completely sincere with yourself that you will actually be able to see every aspect of your life— the good, the bad and the ugly. Be quiet and discover your true self.

"Observing yourself is the necessary starting point for any real change."

—Chalmers Brothers

2. Realise who you truly are, not who you want to be.

You probably already have an idea of who you desperately want to be, but it might not be who you were really designed to be; this is why knowing your real self is so important. When you're aware of who you are, you will then see where you and your specific gifts fit into the bigger picture.

Although there are many points along your journey to help you discover yourself, the best way to begin is to take a personality test and the StrengthsFinder test. Of course, these self-evaluations aren't perfect, but they do pinpoint your top areas of strengths, so you can focus on the change you were meant to bring into the world.

3. Find what you are good at (and not good at).

This might be the most difficult step in your self-discovery process, but it's a necessary one. Sure, it takes trial and error to find what you're good at, and you shouldn't give up before you've had more than enough attempts, but knowing when to quit is a gift that everyone needs to learn.

Quit when you've put in enough time and your efforts aren't yielding the expected return. What is ample time? Only you can define that. But when you quit correctly, it isn't called giving up, it's called making room for something better. When your actions do nothing except draining you—rather than produce more passion and increase your drive to do more—that's a good omen that it is time to shift your focus elsewhere. Your strengths will show you who you truly are.

4. Find what you are passionate about.

Following passion of any kind is a good thing, and you need to pay attention when it comes because it indicates an area of life that you need to devote more attention to. If we're talking about following your passion in work, it's a good thing. And if we're talking about having more passion for life, it's a good thing. Focus more on passion; understand yourself in better ways, and you'll make a bigger impact. Passion produces effort and repeated effort ultimately produces results.

5. Ask for feedback.

As with business enterprises, and political campaigns, feedback plays a huge role in knowing the grey areas that need to be worked on, as well as the brilliant areas that need to be consolidated upon.

If you don't know yourself, listening what others have to say about you is a helpful practice. Ask them two simple questions: "What strengths do you think I need to develop further?" and "What weaknesses do you think I need to work on?" Of course, their opinion isn't going to be perfect, but their feedback will probably indicate a few areas you should at least take a second look at. This step is especially important for those who are stuck in discovering themselves. Sometimes those closest to us can see something we might not be able to see in ourselves. Remember most times, people see the specks in other people's eyes but not the ones in theirs.

6. Assess your relationships.

A big aspect of knowing yourself can be found in your relationships. When you realise the simple fact that you'll never truly know anyone else until you discover yourself; the importance of knowing yourself becomes even more glaring. This truth especially rings true for business leaders, because if you don't know the people on your team, then you will be lost as a leader. But this rule also applies to any relationship in your life. Almost as much as you need to know yourself, other people also need to know who you are. People need you—the real you.

Use your reflections to fight your biggest fears, because when you understand who you are meant to be, your purpose will finally become bigger than your fears. When you realise who you are, you will spend less time and energy spinning your wheels. Focusing on your strengths gives you the needed traction to begin making a better and bigger difference in the world. When you know yourself, you will find more peace, and you achieve success quicker than ever before.

7. Strengthen your mind.

Self-confidence is a state of mind that can be attained through deliberate action. Apportioning time (preferably an hour per day) to nurture your body, mind and spirit can be done in different ways. You may meditate, read and exercise in the morning. If you're not creating time for yourself, then you're allowing someone or something extraneous to shape your view of the world.

8. Discard the negative thoughts you don't need.

A whole new branch of psychology is dedicated to mindfulness, but it boils down to this: Negative thoughts and insecurities pop up like pimples. And, like pimples, picking at them even if you mean to discredit and burst that negative bubble, ultimately worsens it. So, mindfulness practice teaches you to treat thoughts as tools. Use and consolidate on the ones you need, while you do away with the ones you don't.

9. Live a lifestyle of personal growth.

Engaging yourself in courses or professional relationships that force you to grow ensures that you're always growing, which in turn generates confidence and humility. From therapeutic programs to physical programs, to leadership programs, committing to this kind of regular growth by showing up and being fully present, are the keys to confidence.

10. Learn about impostor syndrome.

Many experts and professionals will at some point experience a psychological phenomenon known as imposter syndrome, complete with feelings of inadequacy and a fear that everything accomplished to date has been through sheer luck and not a product of their hardwork and dexterity. To surmount this, learn to internalise accomplishments and make them a part of you. Peer groups provide a great avenue to talk it out and build confidence.

11. Dress for success.

No matter what level of business you're in, it's important to dress for the kind of client you want, rather than the one you have. There's this idea of working from home in PJs. The most successful people get up early and dress like they're off for a day at the office, and it's shown in their attitude. When you look good, you feel good and you're more confident, too.

12. Take an improv class.

Improv classes make you think on your toes in front of an audience. Being on stage helps build and grow your confidence as being in front of crowds teaches you how to think and react quickly spontaneously—all things that translate well to a boardroom or public speaking avenue.

13. Produce a high- quality personal brand.

A key component to building self-confidence is in publicly building one's brand. This can be done through the creation of high-quality content like blog posts, e-books, podcasts or video content. Even if it doesn't receive much traction initially, the fact that you have a body of work that you are proud to refer others to can make a big difference in your self-confidence.

Recognise your value outside of your work.

Your self-confidence needs to be firmly rooted in who you are outside of your success in your political campaign. So, find ways to get connected with yourself and grow. Perhaps volunteer, work out, read, hang out with friends, do pro-bono work; whatever it takes for you to see your value irrespective of how well you're doing professionally.

Learn how to defend yourself and belief

Whether you feel lacking in this area or just want to strengthen your belief for the extra benefits, try these ideas to further develop your self-belief:

Have confidence in your own abilities to get something done

Be your own best supporter and encourage yourself to get your tasks done. Learn to break down your challenges into small steps until you're confident that you can handle them.

Let's say Mr. D's business was struggling. Mr. D knew what he wanted to achieve in the long run but he lacked confidence in his ability to make it happen. So, instead of being overwhelmed by the big picture, he devised a means of getting things done. He got into the habit of setting 90 day plans to bring himself closer to achieving the big goal. He would then break the 90 day plan down into monthly targets and finally, daily actions. He could then focus on the daily actions which he had enough confidence to pursue.

Having faith in yourself can be an arduous task especially when you are facing a big and daunting goal but when you break it down into bite size actions, it becomes so much easier.

Create dreams

Whether it's getting the career you want, getting more training, meeting someone you admire, traveling to a faraway place, or setting a goal to save a million dollars; never forget to connect with your dreams.

We often get dissuaded from pursuing our dreams because we don't believe in our ability to make them come to fruition. What we fail to take note of is that it takes time to achieve a big goal/dream. In the time it takes to achieve that goal/dream, you also have the time to acquire the knowledge, skills and attitudes required to achieve it. Don't base your beliefs in tomorrow's success on the abilities you possess today. Have faith in your ability to learn and grow.

Establish goals and go for the gold

Having faith in yourself means you're motivated to get things done. Get into the habit of setting goals (both short-term and long-term). Then, you can embark on active steps to get them done. With every goal that you achieve, no matter how little, your confidence level increases. Believing in yourself is not attained by a stroke of luck; it comes from building a track record of achievement. That track record starts with setting goals.

Treat yourself well

Treating yourself with a nurturing nature and the knowledge that you're a deserving human being is a core aspect of developing belief in yourself.

As you start to see yourself as worthy of being treated with respect, others will also begin to get that message too. For those who don't get that message, you will come to the realisation that they deserve no place in your life.

Treat yourself with respect and care and then demand that others treat you the same way.

Ensure motivation is high

Remember the childhood tale about the little engine that could? When you want to accomplish your tasks with relative ease and excellence to achieve your goals, it's an incredible proof of your level of motivation. Build momentum to fuel your motivation.

To ensure you stay motivated for your biggest goals, take the time to understand why you want to achieve these goals. You should also regularly take the time to picture your life as it will be once you have achieved the set goals i.e. how you will be live with the benefits.

The age-long saying that where there is a will there is a way is very apt and true. When you reinforce your motivation, like this, you will create an insurmountable will to achieve your goal and you will carve a way to make it happen. Such is the power of having faith in yourself.

During the tough times, keep the faith

"When the going gets tough, the tough gets going."

Joseph P. Kennedy

No one is exempted from experiencing rocky chapters in their life. We all as human beings are vulnerable to experiencing bad and not too savoury moments in our life. But if you believe in yourself, you can meet those challenging phases with a positive mindset and solid fortitude. You'll move through the trying moments, push forward, and know you'll come out on the other side as a smarter, stronger and surer version of yourself.

During the tough times, remind yourself of how you have gotten through tough times before. Think about how you had the resilience and toughness to get through it. Summon that resilient spirit and you will soon find yourself starting to fight back.

Focus on what you can engage in on a daily basis to emerge stronger on the other side of the cliff. Your confidence level will be raised as you take each step, but you must start with some self-belief.

Recognise the bounty you have

Irrespective of what stage of life you're living, search for the good that surrounds you. Get the most you can out of each moment. Live in the moment and be determined to focus on and, be thankful for all the things that are going for you in your life.

When you are feeling down it is very tempting to think that your life is completely bad but that is usually not the case. Learn to delineate different aspects of your life from each other i.e. If one area of your life is not working, don't automatically assume that every area of your life is in a bad state; keep your sense of disappointment restricted to the area where you are underperforming.

Then channel your energy to each area of your life and spend a little time being appreciative for all the good things in your life, e.g. if you are struggling at work you may remind yourself of your successes such as:

Your political ambition

Your affectionate partner and kids

Your great friends

Your achievement at the gym

Your ability to look after your health

You could be filled with gratitude for anything positive in your life. The important thing is that you take the time to identify the positives and appreciate them.

Also, don't wait for something to go wrong before you find something in your life to be grateful for. Take a little time each day to be grateful and whenever you achieve any success in your life, no matter how small, celebrate it.

Having faith in yourself is a choice and one of the most powerful choices you could ever maket. In the face of adversity, any of the seven steps outlined above, can prove daunting but they are choices which you can make. If you dedicate yourself to nurturing self-belief and set aside a little time each day for working on it; you will soon realise that you possess greater resilience when the tough times come. You will stand strong, safe in the knowledge that no matter what life throws at you, you will be able to face and surmount it. Practise these strategies and you'll discover the sheer joy and comfort of knowing you can do whatever it is you choose when you have faith in yourself.

Practise being transparent and authentic.

It might seem difficult at times, but if you learn to openly and honestly express yourself, it will feel like a weight has been lifted off your shoulders. So often, we hide behind a nod and a halfhearted smile instead of saying what we think. It takes practice, but learning to be genuine and open about what you are feeling or thinking is the first step. Once you get in the habit of making yourself heard without being overly defensive or accommodating, people will be more open to hearing you.

Take small but powerful steps.

If you are grappling with being assertive, start taking small steps to be able to stand up for yourself. Merely learning to walk more confidently—head held up high, shoulders back—will help you appear and feel more confident. Positively channel that confidence when dealing with others. This attitude can be applied to all areas of your life. Feeling annoyed at the person who cut in front of you on the queue at Starbucks? Politely ask them to move to the back. See an unfair charge on a bill from one of your service providers? Call and contest the unfair charge.

When someone attacks, wait them out.

As you grow more confident in expressing yourself, you're also going to have to learn to stand up to those who want to take you for a ride. There will always be people whose personalities are set to attack mode by default. It's pertinent that you remain calm but assertive if you feel like someone is trying to intimidate you. Don't allow yourself to get frazzled or react with blows below the belt. Don't mind them or allow them to browbeat you either. Walk the high road but firmly stand your ground.

Figure out what's really bothering you.

Going with the flow for the purposes of not making waves actually creates more anxiety and stress for yourself. Of course, summoning the courage to face something or someone that is bothering you can feel scary. But facing the issue will empower you to make it better and diminishes the control it has over you. Remember, people can't access your mind; if you don't voice out what is bothering you, no one will know.

Clarify first, without attacking.

It's quite tempting to take a self-righteous stand, particularly if you are sure you are right. From your perspective, you are justifiably defending yourself against someone who seems to be entirely wrong. But it's also quite important to resist the urge to react with emotion. Rather than reacting with emotions, take a breath and calmly explain your perspective to them. Avoid combative tones or words that are potentially accusative. Clarify exactly what you mean and listen to their response. Only then can a real discussion begin to take place.

Practice makes perfect.

Once you start getting a grip on what it means to stand up for yourself, it's time to practise asking for what you want as often as possible. When someone says something you openly disagree with, or you feel pushed into doing something you don't want to do, speak up. Research has shown that it takes 66 days to form a new habit, so stick with the new assertiveness for two months and you might be surprised by the results.

Be deliberate.

Here's a situation that many of us have at one time or the other found ourselves in; sharing space with a messy colleague or a roommate who is lazy. You might have remained silent while growing more aggravated at the situation. It might be tempting to slip into a passively-aggressive behavior, such as angrily cleaning up the mess or making derisive comments. Try being deliberate instead. Tell the person how you are feeling without sounding accusatory. Be straightforward with your concerns. Follow this up with a simple suggestion that can correct the situation, such as: "If you took a minute to tidy up your space at night, it would be a big help."

Stand up for your time.

Time is a limited and precious commodity, and yet

we often feel pressured to just give it away when we have the ability to say no. There are times when you might be left with little or no choice, such as when your boss says a project has high priority. But don't let these obligations dictate how you spend the hours of your day. You are in control of your own time. Push back when it's appropriate, or smartly disengage from those people or situations that unnecessarily crowd your schedule.

Recognise that no one can invalidate you.

You are in complete control of your feelings and actions. Your thoughts, emotions, beliefs and ideas belong to you, and no one else can tell you what you feel or vitiate your opinions. Likewise, if you seek to vitiate the point of view or perspective of others, you are also sabotaging any chance for problem-solving or having an open discussion.

Find the right balance

Learning to stand up for yourself won't happen overnight. It takes time to grow comfortable with being assertive. While you are in the early stage of learning to stand up for yourself, it might help to assume that you are an actor learning to play a new role.

Assume that you are the most assertive person you have ever come in contact with. How would they handle themselves in a difficult situation? There might be times when you swing from being overly enthusiastic to being too indecisive. Learning to stand up for yourself is like riding a bike; eventually you will find the right balance.

Strategies to Make Great Decisions in Life

Do you feel stuck in any area of your life? Are you too frightened to take the necessary steps to advance your health, wealth, relationships and career?

Do you want to make life changing choices that will move you in the direction of your dreams continually?

If your answer to any of these questions is yes, it may be time to evaluate your decision-making process. Understanding how the process works is crucial to bypassing significant hurdles along your path to success.

Make better decisions

The crucial role decision making plays in the way events unfold cannot be underestimated. But people don't usually pay much attention to the telling effects of making decisions. Most of us move through life unaware of what thoughts we're thinking and what actions we're taking.

However, the decisions we make daily, create our own personal reality. And our decisions shape who we are as individuals.

Most of us are inclined to make decisions based on low self-esteem, fear, and a lack of willpower.

So rather than making bold moves, we end up stuck in our comfort zone.

• **Goal achievement**

Fortunately, it has been scientifically proven that it is possible to reprogram your brain for higher levels of consciousness. So, if you're not satisfied with the way things are turning out in your life right now, making a concerted effort towards moving out of our comfort zone—in order to make better decisions—will be crucial to being the person you want to be and creating the life you want to have in the future.

When you make reasonable effort towards taking control of your health, lifestyle and wealth, in a positive way, you activate four neurological processes. These processes which *Mark Waldman*, the co-author of *Neuro Wisdom: The New Brain Science of Money, Happiness and Success*, refer to as the "4 Pillars of Wealth". They are:

Motivation: When you become aware of what uniquely spurs you, you can consciously choose the activities that will bring the greatest success.

Decision-making: Once you are motivated to acquire or do something, your brain activates circuits in the frontal lobes to start making decisions. This process can be disrupted by stress, worry, and doubt. But you can train your mind to stay focused, confident, and optimistic.

Creativity: Using the powers of your unique creative imagination, you will solve problems faster and thus increase your productivity.

Awareness: The process of mindful self-reflection can augment self-awareness, social awareness, and spiritual awareness, giving your life more meaning and purpose. You will also arouse your brain's circuitry for empathy, morality and compassion.

Each of the four pillars above is pivotal for goal achievement and success. And if you jettison any of them, you'll likely limit your ability to build both inner and outer wealth and achievement.

Let's emphasise a little more on the second of the four pillars: decision-making. Here are some strategies to help you make better decisions:

1. Use both sides of your brain.

What is the first step in the decision-making process? Well, when making a big decision, feel empowered to use the two sides of your brain (instead of just your logical, left side). It's also important to find the balance between emotion and reason.

The right brain, our emotional intelligence, is inherently linked to our behavior and conduct as well as the important decisions we make throughout our lifetime.

Both your decision-making and idea creating processes begin in your left prefrontal cortex, and if there isn't enough emotion behind these processes, the part of the brain called the nucleus accumbens (NAc) doesn't activate. If the NAc isn't activated, dopamine (the feel-good neurotransmitter that recognises reward) won't be discharged into your body, and you'll likely remain unstimulated back in your comfort zone. And decisions made from the comfort zone rarely end up being beneficial to you in the long run.

2. Visualise your future, successful self.

If you want to know how to make successful decisions, take a moment to think about what success means to you. How do you define personal success? Pen your answer down in a journal or on a piece of paper.

Next, visualise your ideal, future self. Do this by getting into a calm position, close your eyes, and allow your mind stray into a daydream.

What do you see and feel? Are you bright with energy? Do you have a radiant glow about you? Are you in the best shape ever? Are you in love? Do you have a fun community and a supportive circle of friends? Are you financially autonomous? Do you get along well with your business partners, colleagues, and employees? Take notes, if you like.

Creative Visualisation is a crucial strategy for those of us on the path of great success. When you have a positive mental image and see yourself as a successful person, you begin to believe you're capable of perfect health, happiness, and wealth. Seeing as they say is believing, right? And you must believe in order for you to achieve.

3. Recognise the power behind each decision you make.

Before making a decision, you have to understand the effects of the choices you make. Any decision that you make has a ripple effect and causes a chain of events to happen.

For example, if a company you'd love to work requires you do a presentation for key stakeholders before you're employed and you decide not to go through with it because you have an inherent fear of public speaking, that decision might result in you missing out on an opportunity to have your own multi-million dollar company in the future.

In this case, it all boils down to first making the solemn decision to overcome your fear of public speaking, so you can do what you love, have a sense of fulfilment and be financially independent for the rest of your life.

4. Go with your gut.

When you find yourself having difficulties choosing from multiple options, your gut is one of your most powerful decision-making tools. To hone in on your gut feeling, stop for a moment and don't think about the advantages and disadvantages. Simply sit in a quiet place and observe what feelings come to the surface.

Do you feel tight in the chest area? Or an open lightness in your heart? Do you feel relief? Excitement? What other physical sensations do you feel?

Research shows that our instincts often first hit us on a splanchnic level, telling us what we need to know well before our consciousness catches up. A Neuroscientist and one of the world's leading and formost authority on human consciousness, Dr. Joel Pearson, recently discovered that intuition does in fact exist.

Pearson and his research team have demonstrated that unconscious emotions enhance the speed and precision of decision-making—a discovery that could prove important for investigations into how conscious and unconscious information combine to shape and influence behaviors.

When making big decisions, you've got to dig into your inner sagacity. The best ancient advice for figuring out what you truly want is to look within yourself.

So, before making any major moves, take some time to delve into that "funny" feeling. You've most likely had a hunch before; a hint that steered you in the right direction? That right there is your sixth sense communicating with you. Pay attention to it.

5. Don't ask other people what you should do.

You don't have to ask people what they think. It becomes even more difficult to decide when you are caught up in other people's opinions about what's best for you. (This does not necessarily mean you shouldn't seek advice or expert opinion when the need arises.)

If you ask four people what they think you should do, you will most likely get four different pieces of advice. And the feedback will likely lead to confusion and second guessing.

Feel free to consult the people who will be directly affected by your decision and then confidently let everyone know what you've decided.

6. Ask yourself the right questions.

Once you know how you feel about the decision, it's time to ask your brain the right questions: What do I want in my lifetime? Will the outcome of my decision move me closer to what I really want? Does the benefit exceed the cost? Is the risk level worth the reward? How committed am I to this change?

As Dr. David Welch, professor of political science at the University of Waterloo in Ontario and author of *Decisions: The Art of Effective Decision Making*, explains, "People who aren't self-reflective are going to end up making bad decisions because they don't really know what they want in the first place."

7. Align your life with your core values.

The decisions you make based on your core values create motivational alignment. So, make your decisions based on whether or not they align with your highest values, passions, and priorities, or it's not going to feel like you made the right choice.

Before you can figure out if the decision is aligned with the things that mean the most to you, you first need to be clear about what those core values are. Make a written list of your highest values. And once you're clear, draw a list of all the ways your choice aligns (or doesn't align) with those values.

8. Whatever you decide to do, do

Have you ever met an unyielding person you didn't like? Even if you have, weren't you somewhat amazed at their drive to succeed?

When it comes to taking action in your life, you've got to have a strong backbone. So before you start running for election, make sure you're doing something that motivates you to trudge on (despite failure).

"Grit is passion and perseverance for very long-term goals. Grit is having stamina. Grit is sticking with your future, day in, day out come rain come shine, not just for the week, not just for the month, but for years, and working hard to make that future a reality. Grit is living life like it's a marathon that requires the highest level of stamina and not a sprint that requires a sudden gush of adrenaline."

Angela Lee Duckworth

Along with grit, having gusto is an equally important trait of successful people.

You have to be passionate about the life choices you make. There's power in passion. This passion can then be fuelled by a high level of enthusiasm.

Yes, You Can

So when it comes to making the right decision, don't fall back into your comfort zone and stay in a career you can't stand. Find ways to fire up your spirit and take giant leaps toward your dreams.

STEP TO SUCCESS TWO

Do Some Research

Running a campaign is actually quite similar to running a business. Use these tips to create a robust campaign that will drive you to success at the polls!

Within modern businesses, Marketing research can give a business a picture of what kinds of new products and services may yield profit. For products and services already available, marketing research can tell companies whether they are meeting their customers' needs and expectations. By researching the answers to specific questions, small-business owners can learn whether they need to change their package design or tweak their delivery methods, and even whether they should consider offering additional or new services.

"Failure to do market research before you begin a business venture or during its operation is like driving a car from Texas to New York without a map or street signs," says William Bill of Wealth Design Group LLC in Houston. "You have to know which direction to travel and how fast to go. A good market research plan indicates where and who your customers are. It will also tell you when they are most likely and willing to purchase your goods or use your services."

When you conduct marketing research, you can use the results either to generate a business and marketing plan or to measure the success of your current plan. That's why it's pertinent to ask the right questions, in the right way, and of the right people. Research, if done poorly, can navigate a business in the wrong direction. Here are some market-research basics that can help get you started and some mistakes to also avoid:

Types of Market Research

Primary Research: The goal of a primary research is to gather data from analyzing current polls and the effectiveness of current practices. Primary research also takes other competitors' plans into account, giving you necessary information about your competition.

Collecting primary research can include:

- Interviews (either by telephone or face-to-face)
- Surveys (online or by mail)
- Questionnaires (online or by mail)
- Focus groups gathering a sampling of potential voters or donors and getting their direct feedback
- Some important questions might include:
- What indices do you put into consideration when putting your faith in this candidate or

cause?
- What do you like or dislike about current incumbant currently in office?
- What areas would you suggest for improvement?

Secondary Research:

The goal of a secondary research is to analyze data that has already been published. With secondary data, you can pin point competitors, create benchmarks and identify target segments. Your segments are the people who fall into your targeted demographic - people who live a certain lifestyle, exhibit particular behavioral patterns or fall into a predetermined age group.

Collecting Data

No campaign can succeed without understanding its customers, products and services, and the market as a whole similar to understanding an electorate in a campaign. Competition is often tense, and operating without conducting research may give your competitors an advantage over you.

There are two categories of data collection: quantitative and qualitative. Quantitative methods employ mathematical analysis and require a large sample size. The results of this data shed light on statistically relevant differences. One place to find quantitative results if you have a website is in your web analytics. This information can help you discover many things, such as where your website intrerests are coming from, how long visitors are staying on your site and from which page they are exiting.

Qualitative methods help you develop and fine-tune your quantitative research methods. They can help campaigns define problems and often use interview methods to learn about the opinion of constituents, values and beliefs. With qualitative research, the sample size is usually small.

Many new candidates, often short of time and money, try to circumvent these procedures that can later backfire. Here are three potential pitfalls to avoid.

Common Marketing Mistakes

Using only secondary research: Depending on someone else's work or older voting data doesn't give you the full image. It can be a great boulevard to begin, of course, but the information you generate from secondary research can be outdated. You can miss out on other factors which is salient to your business.

Using only web resources: When you use common search engines to accumulate information, you get only data that are available to everyone and it may not be fully exact. To perform deeper searches while staying within your budget, use the resources at college campus, small-business center or your local library.

Inspecting only the people you know: Candidates sometimes interview only family members and close colleagues when conducting research, but friends and family are often not the best survey subjects. You need to talk to real constituents about their needs, wants and expectations before you can get the most useful and accurate information

General Steps in the Research Process

Step 1

Create your research objectives by describing, in detail, what is to be achieved by your research in order to systematically acquire the data to answer the research question or solve the problem.

Step 2

Decide on a research generalship that provides the most cost effective method of gathering information and manufacture the best possible answers to the research question. Some of these generalships include sample research, statistical analysis, correlation, and quantified data like mathematical models. Other methods are similar to the field of anthropology where data is collected through participant observation and focus-group interviews found in psychological investigations. Don't worry too much an this as your Camapign Manager is likely to lead on what type of research is most valuable to your campaign.

Step 3

Identify the research sample or subjects of your study and begin to gather the primary or secondary data needed to meet your research objectives. The methods of data collection will vary but are not limited to: taking part in a social situation and recording the findings publicly or secretly observing the behaviors of subjects, interviewing subjects one at a time or in groups, supervising a questionnaire to survey the attitudes of your sample population reviewing documents of other sources

Step 4

All in all, the construction of the data is not enough and is insignificant if we are unable to relate them to structured and logical explanations, thus leading your results to fully formulated constituent research.

Opposition Research

Channel your emotion, accept what you can't control, take the offensive – use your competition to your best advantage.

Whether it's a business competitor or a political opponent, the answer to what is holding us back often lies within the hurdle itself.

Instead of sulking at what stands in our way of achieving our goals, we should change our views and see the problem with a ready solution. These solutions can be found in time-defying set of philosophical principles that great men and women have followed.

An opponent is nothing more than a guide that will show us the way to defeat our hurdles, or how to go around them. Here are seven strategies to turn those that stand in our way into the way:

Channel Your Energy

Instead of giving in to frustration, we can put it to good use. It can power our actions, which, unlike our disposition, become stronger and better when loose and bold. We can respond by resisting, or we can channel our energy in a way that empowers and strengthens us.

To survive segregation in the 1950s and 1960s, Arthur Ashe learned from his father to hide his emotions and feelings on the court. No reacting, no getting upset at missed shots, and no challenging bad calls.

All the energy and emotion he had to suppress was channeled into a better venture. It produced a bold and graceful playing form. While his face was controlled, his body was alive; fluid, brilliant, and all over the court.

Feelings need an outlet to flow out, of course, but Ashe deployed them to fuel his explosive speed, in his slams, forehands, groundstrokes, chips and dives.

Misfortune can harden you. Or it can loosen you up and make you better, if you let it. Rename it and claim it - that's exactly what Ashe did.

It's a power that drives our opponents and rivals nuts. They think we're toying with them. It's maddening – like we aren't even trying, like we've tuned out the world. Like we're exempted from external stressors and limitations on the march towards our goals.

Love Everything That Happens

When we do away with our expectations and accept what happens to us, understanding that certain things, particularly bad things, are outside our control, we are left with this: loving whatever happens to us and facing it with unfailing cheerfulness.

It is the act of turning what we must do into what

we get to do.

Instead of counteracting what we can't control, we can channel our energy and emotions and exertions where they will have real impact. This is that place. We will tell ourselves: This is what I've got to do or put up with? Well, I might as well be happy about it.

It's a little unnatural to have a feeling of gratitude for things we never wanted to happen in the first place, but the opportunities and benefits actually lie within adversity. In surmounting them, we can emerge empowered, stronger and sharper. There is little reason to delay these feelings. To reluctantly acknowledge later that it was for the best, when we could have felt that earlier because it was inevitable.

What's Right Is What Works

We expend a lot of time thinking about how things are supposed to be, or what the rules dictate that we should do, trying to get it all perfect. We tell ourselves that we'll get started once the conditions are perfect, or once we're sure we can put faith in this or that. When, really, it'd be better for us to focus on making do with what we've got – on focusing on results instead of pretty methods.

Sometimes you do it this way, sometimes the other way, not deploying the strategies you learned in school but shoehorning them to fit each and every situation. Any way that works – that's the motto.

As they say in Brazilian jiu-jitsu, it doesn't matter how you get your opponents to the ground after all, what matters is that you take them down.

You have your mission on your hand, whatever it is. Like the rest of us, you're in the pinch between the way you wish things were and the way they actually are (which always seems to be a disaster). How far are you willing to go? What risks are you willing to take?

Quit complaining: No waffling. No submitting to powerlessness or fear. How are are you going to solve this problem? How are you going to bypass the rules that hold you back?

Use Your Opponent Against Themselves

Wise men are able to make a fitting use even of their enemies.

–Plutarch

Sometimes you surmount hurdles not by attacking them headlong but by withdrawing into your cocoon and letting them come at you. You can use the actions of others against them instead of acting yourself.

We sometimes get so immersed with forging ahead

that we forget that there are other ways to get where we are heading. It doesn't naturally occur to us that standing still, or in some cases, even going backward, might actually be the best way to advance and progress to the next level.

There is a certain level of humility needed in this approach. It means accepting the fact that the way you originally wanted to do things is impossible. You just haven't got it in you to do it the "traditional" way. But so what? There are other ways to do it.

We should find solace in this. It means that very few hurdles are ever too big for us. Because that bigness might in fact be an added advantage. Because we can use that bigness against the obstacle itself; turning the obstacle against itself. Remember, a castle can be an intimidating, impregnable fortress, or it can be turned into an inhibiting prison when surrounded. The difference is simply a shift in action and approach.

We can use the things that block us to our own advantage, making them do the difficult work for us. Sometimes this means leaving the obstacle as it is, instead of trying so hard to change it.

Use The Flank Attack

A study of 30 conflicts consisting more than 280 campaigns from ancient history to modern history, came to the astounding conclusion that only six victories of the 280 campaigns were a product of a direct attack on the enemy's main army. Only six. That's a meager 2%.

If not from frontal assault, where then do we find victory?

From everywhere else: Right from the psychological to the unexpected. From attacking from the flanks to drawing opponents out of their defenses and even to the untraditional. Quite aptly from anything.

The way that works isn't always the most impressive. Sometimes, it even feels like you're circumventing things or punching below the belt. There's a lot of pressure to try to match people move for move, strategy for strategy, attack for attack, as if sticking with what works for you is somehow cheating. Let me save you the burden of guilt and self-flagellation: It's not.

Seize The Offensive

The best men are not those who have waited for chances but who have taken them; besieged chance, conquered the change, and made chance the servitor.

–E.H. Chapin

Ordinary people avoid negative situations and avoid trouble. What great people do is the direct opposite. They never waste an opportunity to turn a personal disaster or crisis to their advantage.

At certain moments in our respective brief existences, we are faced with great tribulations. We must see that this "problem" doesn't just come and go without presenting an opportunity for a solution that we have long been waiting for.

When people believe we are down and out, that is exactly when we should spring up and prove the doubters wrong

In many battles, as in life, the two opposing forces will often reach a point of mutual exhaustion. It's the one who rises the next morning after a long day of fighting and rallies, instead of retreating – the one who says, I intend to attack and whip them right here and now – who will carry victory home.

Get Moving

Life can be frustrating. Oftentimes we know what our problems are. We may even know what to do about them. But we fear that taking action is too risky, that we don't have the experience or that it's not how we pictured it or because it's too expensive, because it's too soon, because we think something better might come along, because it might not work.

And you know what happens as a result? Nothing. We do nothing.

Tell yourself: The time for that has passed. The wind is rising. The bell's been rung. Get started, get moving.

So when you're frustrated in pursuit of your own goals, don't sit there and complain that you don't have what you want or that this obstacle won't budge. If you haven't even tried yet, then of course you will still be in the exact same place. You haven't actually pursued anything.

All the greats we admire started by saying, "Yes, let's go." And they usually did it in less desirable circumstances than we'll ever suffer.

Just because the conditions aren't exactly to your liking, or you don't feel ready yet, doesn't mean you get a pass. If you want momentum, you'll have to create it yourself, right now, by getting up and getting started.

Know your opposition before your opposition knows You

Handling opposition

It is entirely natural to have opposition. Opponents stretch thinking, pressure test proposals and balance the corporate agenda. Without opposition, you may end up with an organisation being dominated by a powerful few; and this can wreak havoc on the strategy, results and morale at least in the medium term.

Yet, desirable though it is, the fact remains that the opposition will still want to win. They may be mature and tell you that it is all about making the right decision for the business, but don't be fooled. Underneath the rhetoric is a real person. They, like you, much prefer to be the one driving the agenda and prevailing in the cut and thrust of political life.

And there are certain things they hope you never learn how to do because they can help you to beat them. Things such as:

How to Discover Their Strategy.

Although the steps they are taking right now may be apparent, what is really going on behind the scenes, the moves they are making and the contingencies they have in place will be a closely guarded secret. What can you do to discover more?

How to Identify Their Weak Points.

Sure, they may put on a front of sharing their objective assessment of the pros and cons of each option, but chances are they are carefully managing the message around their vulnerabilities. Watch closely for the clues and do a little hypothesis testing to learn more.

How to Present a Balanced Case.

Plausibly one of their main pleasures is watching you present a biased case, only presenting the benefits and the outcomes which might default from backing your proposals. They are aware nobody will totally believe you.

How to Marshall the Masses.

Make your way into social domain of organisations. Chances are, if they are a mighty opponent, they have succeeded better than others at becoming the trusted adviser to the powerful. They direct much atttentions at a few to the detriment of many. Yet we have seen huge benefit can be gained by weight of numbers, or is it wisdom of crowds? They won't want you to acknowledge that.

How to Manage the Airtime.

Organisational life takes time as it demands utter commitment. If you could device a way out to manage the exposure better than the opposition, they may at the end be found longing to be called into the executive meeting until after it has ended. "Sorry, we didn't get around to your item."

How to Unleash the Passion.

They may attract your attention with the idea that careful consideration of the facts and logic helps to decide, but will hide that the actual influence is gained by motivational appeals. They'll do that quietly while you are unwary.

If you can practice these, you will dramatically improve your strength to give the resistant party a real run for their money. You can concentrate your attentions on these areas for your ideas, your proposals, your outcomes, and your career, can shift in status for good.

Analysing your Competition

The cool calculation of your competitors weaknesses is a bit tasking on the web.

So many successful players in the internet marketing fold reflect the growing goodness in competitive marketing analysis. What this tit-bit showcases is that to win on the web is now a thing of necessity than ever.

Healthy vying and rivalry is fast becoming an essential fabric for success in this jet age and in marketing led businesses. The success mantra has evolved necessarily over the last few years, especially considering the emergence of many game changers, such as Google, Facebook and Twitter.

This is how the these days' internet marketing practices changed, and competitive analysis schemes employed traditionally aren't exactly as effective contemporarily as they were in the past.

Competition analysis – Essential for your campaign

Competition stresses better emphasis on perfection in your niche service fold. Success and expertise excellence thrive on a stout and hearty competition, which is why having the knowledge of your rivals remains crucial to contemporary marketing orchestrations. Further, without a thorough comparison model and affective analysis, it is difficult to know whether your marketing strategy is yielding outstanding dividends or driving your hard earned marketing budget into aught.

An active competition watch kills two birds with a single stone. First it assists with better understanding of competitor tactics and second it helps you to see your own problem areas. More so, I'm sure you'd comply knowing where you stand at the moment is very crucial.

1. Campaign Tone

Estimate constituent engagement signs for success/loss, such as knowing their campaign tone, for example, peppiness implies doggedness, commitment implies practicality and orthodoxical approach posits they are afraid to try new things.

Look for attitudinal patterns and campaign redefining and altering (overly frequently means campaign failure, while occasional changes imply a campaign is working effectively.)

2. Investigate their constituent acquisition approach

Look for opponents' social media engagement – how frequently they attend to the voters, are their social media reps doing a proper job or not and subtle indicators of customer acquisition via self upliftment. For example – "Candidate A celebrates 500+ social media followers with a campaign rally and givaway this weekend"

3. How actively are they using social media and for what purpose?

Social media drives are diverse as we go from Facebook, Twitter, and Google+ to Instagram or Pinterest. Hence, try to find the course behind each one of them along with the usual objective.

4. What to know about your opponent and where?

This is a juncture where you really need to grasp that a candidate is not your competitor online if they don't offer their views via the internet. Your competitors based online could be entirely vary. Weigh new and emerging players in the market.

Use tracking tools such as Google Alerts, Talkwalker, Mention, and so forth.

Evaluate the reason of your rivals – if you share similitude ground, look for areas where a certain edge can be established and tuned.

Search and discover areas that your competitors are exploiting fine. It could be a service gap, untapped audience section or anything that is bolstering your rival's footing. Prepare a note of it and begin to work at your end.

Gauging performance of your peers is almost as crucial as analysing your own campaigns. It is important to take the habitude that your competition is analysing your business and taking plans from your hard work and that the tables need to be balanced.

Everyone should have an opponent. It is natural to be excited. If you don't have opposition, you are not there, or you are deluded. Building proper tenacity and displaying the right level of resolve may not win the day, but it should win the respect of those you are attempting to influence.

The definition of tenacity, which seems most proper when it comes to effect in the workplace, is "persistence of purpose". Vigor is the ability to display commitment to what you believe in. You keep picking yourself up, dusting yourself off, and sharply get going again having learned a little more.

SECTION TWO
Getting Ready to Run

STEP TO SUCCESS THREE

Make A Budget

Creating an effective budget that lasts can be a stumbling block. Let's be realistic. Budgets can be tasking and demanding and they require a lot of concentration.

In fact, a budget is a necessary part of a campaign financial schema.

Don't give up on your budget.

You can find satisfaction on any earning and you will be fine on a budget. Your budget is the foundation upon which your financial life is constructed. Think of it as your foundation. It's your scheme for spontaneity. Your plan for the unforeseen financial rollercoaster life hands you. It will aid you to cope with financial constraints.

And, an working and efficient budget will take you only one to two hours a month to manage.

These are the initial ways to create a budget. It's a process, but glady there is no such thing as a failed budget. This will lead you to financial buoyancy, so be hopeful:

Yes, You Can

1. Write down your financial goals.

Having goals is needed to tracking your progress

Your goals perhaps have to do with political campaign, debt lib, building savings, or utmost generosity. Whatever they are, ruminate on your short term and long term goals. Write them down. These are your financial motivators.

2. Record every single purchase you make, without exception.

Think of this as your budget prep.

No dollar should escape accountability. Record every dollar that leaves your pocket. Underestimating your expenses will be ultimately disastrous for you. Knowing your spending habits will put you on the right track.

Create your spending categories.

In addition, to the above, list all larger non-monthly expenses (mailers, unexpected trips, campaigns consumables).

Don't forget a "fun money" or miscellaneous category. You need to give yourself some breathing room.

Hold a budget meeting (yes, with your spouse, campaign partners).

Budgeting could be regarded in this wise as the gathering of likely minds. It's about healthy negotiation, compromise and respect. This is where you will be able to determine how much resources in dollars should be allocated to each of the spending categories.

This meeting ought to be brief (and friendly).

Design time for your budget creation.

Determine the budget format and tools you are to put into consideration in beginning your budget.

Think about your personality. You could put any of the following into consideration in doing that: pencil and paper, software, envelopes, dry erase board, whatever. Just make it intimately and, preferably, cheap.

Steps to Building a Winning Campaign Budget

Building a campaign budget can surely be said to be one of the first steps to starting your campaign. Without the acknowledgement of how much money you'll need to fundraise, and where it'll all go once you have it, being the comptroller of the ins and outs of financing your campaign can be tricky.

A campaign budget will help you find out where to spend your money, how much you'll need, and the ways forwards with fundraising. It's your first step to managing your resources as effectively as possible and guiding the campaign activities.

Building a great fundraising operation is of utmost importance, and having a well funded campaign budget can fetch you the much needed edge over competing candidates. Your opponent could have wicked resources, but if they are not effected appropriately, it is all a waste. Spending money strategically goes hand in hand with raising money effectively, and it'll timelessly pay off more valuably to your campaign in the long run. The following are the necessary steps to building a winning campaign budget:

1. Create a budget before your start fundraising

Budgeting is the most important part of your campaign finance scheme of action. While you may be eager to jump right into fundraising, a well-researched and well-informed budget is incredibly needed especially at the on-set of your campaign.

Having the know-how on how to efficiently utilise your resources, and how much of it you'll need, is cucial for the attainment of success of your campaign. Your campaign budget should be based on your campaign scheme, and the number of voters you need to reach out to, and how you're planning to disseminate all the necessary items of information that need reaching them on time. If you know how to effectively use your money, it will make things much easier down the line.

2. Have a plan, but be flexible.

Writing a scheme for your budget is necessary, but it's also vital to be able to be dynamic when problems or unforeseen circumstances arise. A budget should be a guideline for your fundraising and spending, suitable and ever-morphing, depending on your needs and your bottom line at any given time. Dynamism means knowing where to direct extra funds or cut funding, depending on your fundraising performance, to use your money most efficiently.

3. Use the 70% rule

In the course of making your campaign budget, try and recollect this rule of thumb: 70% of your budget should be used on voter contact and communications. While there are many factors which will aid effective campaign running, it's cogent not to lose sight of what will win you the election (voters!). This principle or rule leaves 30 percent of the budget for administrative costs, staffing, fundraising, and other overhead spending.

4. Spend money to make money

It might appear counterproductive spending resources upfront before you've done much fundraising, but it's a usual practice to spend a little before you start fundraising. A good quintessences are, when you're planning a campaign, you need to hire field organisers, digital staff, pay for advertising, and buy access to fundraising software, just to name a few of the upfront costs. Services like *Act Blue* and *NGP Van* will likely demand you use resources up front, but they yield huge value when it comes to online fundraising and building your donor lists. Don't overspend, but don't be scared of taking risks committing your resources effectively right at the beginning; you'll need to spend a little to see the largest possible return closer to Election Day.

5. Budget backwards and for absentee & early voters

Factually, the peak interest surrounding a campaign is typically within the time frame of a couple of weeks prior to the election, therefore, make sure to spend most of your money when masses are watching. This is also the time frame when most of your fundraising money will likely come in. Political Action Committee (PAC) money always comes in last and at this point your campaign would have likely gained momentum around the race. Spend what they need to upfront and well before Election Day to build momentum and encourage support, but to ramp up spending on advertising and voter communications when voters either have their ballots or are gearing up to go and use the polls.

On that note, it's needed to remember that not everyone votes on Election Day. Be very certain your budget is mindful of absentee and early voters. These votes are important you should be ready to put everything into consideration to lock in these votes before Election D-day. Budgeting for targeted mail pieces and digital advertising to absentee voters will let you directly target the voters which you have to get to before it's too late.

6. Make room for digital in your communications budget.

Digital is a vital part of any effective voter communications plan – it's unlike those areas you might want to risk skipping. While many components of digital are free, like social media pages, it's important to utilise resources on digital advertising that's actively focusing the voters that matter in your election. Digital used alongside other communications methods such as mail, radio, and TV will affect a distinguishing impact.

Successful Budgeting for a Political Campaign

Kicking off an election campaign would be a walk in the park with proper plans effected. Right after you decide to run for election, the planning phase starts. Once you have announced your candidacy and start bringing in members to run the campaign, there comes two vital functions. One is working on the campaign's communication strategy and the second is being actively involved in a budget for the entire campaign.

Pending on the communication methodologies and staff you'd need, you can work on the budget for your campaign.

Remember that the purpose of the campaign is to win votes. Your budget should aid the steps to reach out to the expected number of voters to put you ahead in the race. The amount of money you end up spending does not matter; what matters is how many voters will ger around the money.

What the budget includes

Let's consider what campaign functions and materials you should include in your budget.

Operations

  Office space

  Office supplies

  Fees and extra charges

  Salaries

  Consulting charges

  Voter files and databases

Website expenses

Polling and research

Voter communication

Direct mail

Literature and paraphernalia

Yard signs

Phone banking

Radio ads

Digital ads

Volunteer expenses

Newspaper ads

Events, meetings etc.

GOTV expenses

Fundraising

Fundraisers

Donation cards

Forms and letterheads

Postage

Reference for estimating expenses

Unless you have been part of a recent campaign or have past experience in creating a budget, it is herculean to estimate how much each of the above processes is going to cost you. To get a rough estimate, you'll need to look through the budget and expense sheets of previous candidates.

Fortunately for you, these records are not hard to come by. Campaigns for political post have financial disclosure requirements. The documents would be publicly available to collect and would put your upcoming spendings in the ballpark.

Sources for raising campaign financial rescources

The moment you have put everything into consideration about election campaign task in investing with an estimated budget for each, based on past campaign records, you can deduce deciding how you are going to raise the resource for your campaign.

The following are some ways campaigns get financed.

Individual investment by the candidate. This may not be viable for every candidate, but in case, you decide to take this path, put in the resource as a loan. That way you stand to get some of it back when you raise donations.

- PACs / Special interest groups that approve candidates whose policies are in line with what suits them well.
- Major donors of past campaigns have a habit of donating. Discover them via voter lists you purchase.
- Events and mail tend to take up expenses and the returns are variable for each campaign. Campaigns yet go by this manner of interaction.
- Loans you can get or commingle with an affluential personality who staunchly wants to see you win the office to support your course effectively.
- Public funding programs. Some cities and districts have public funding programs to allocate taxpayer resource into campaigns. You have to adhere to the mandated terms to make your campaign qualified for public financing.
- Some services like transport, printing and catering can sometimes be manned by supporters for free.

Factors that affect campaign budget

Depending on the post you are running for and the location, there are some inconsistencies in the budget that you have to regard. Some of these expenses are weighed at the beginning while some are relying upon the assistance you draw or how your interaction plan works out. Here are a few:

Electorate size - Primaries have fewer voters to reach than a general election. A local election campaign will comprise even fewer voters to reach out to.

Opposition – How many rivals are you up against? How close is the competition?

Newcomer vs incumbent – A candidate with a recognised name ID would require to spend less than a first timer to raise their candidate detail.

Voter interaction methods – Your contact methodologies like phonebanking, door-knocking and community events have varying expenses.

Coverage by external sources – Political party approval, chargless press coverage and supporter attitude can cut your spendings also.

Allocating your campaign budget

Cutting your budget among the complete campaign functions is also important. A way of effectively actualising this is by segregating all expenses into two parts: Direct voter contact and overhead.

Direct Voter contact takes care of all that is used

to communicate with the voters. Polls, website, ads and phone banking are all grouped under this category. About 65 – 70% of your total budget should be put in course for direct voter contact expenses.

Overhead covers staff, consulting fees and any other bills you gather from movement or voyaging to renting. Acting safely is very crucial and keeping some part of the budget aside for contingencies in case of any necessity, come the future within the campaign time. Around 10% of the budget should be held for selfsame expenses.

A properly sourced budget plan will see you through the entire campaign with no necessity for taking cheaper, less effective paths. Plan in advance and be in conversance with your campaign manager and consultant to draw a budget which will facilitate the campaign you hope to effect.

STEP TO SUCCESS FOUR

Fundraising

Fundraising events are key components of every political campaign. Like the campaign itself, though, the success of these events pends on cautious planning. To assist you in ensuring your political fundraising event is a winner, here are ten major components that are quite imperative you try and incorporate into your event scheme:

1. Purpose:

Firstly, you have to try and be decisive on the purpose of what you are doing, campaigning to win. Is this really a fundraising event? Or does it have other goals? Perhaps your campaign may be directing a whole lot of attention at money-making at the event, but the exact importance or purpose of bringing the event to reality is to gain publicity, or achieve a new coalition. Many political events have beyond one target. Finding out the contents for your event will depend on knowing what goals you are aiming to achieve.

2. Fundraising Goal:

In collaboration with the candidate, campaign manager, or other key members of the campaign, you must decide what amount of money you plan to raise at the event. If this is truly a fundraising activity, then everything in the event plan will be directed at raising this specific amount of resource. The amount you choose should be what you hope to net, that is, the amount you plan to raise after expenses are deducted.

3. Budget:

Every fundraising event plan should have a perfect budget listing all of the expenses that will be required to hold the event. Your budget should include staff, invitations, space rental, catering, entertainment, transportation, security, utilities, and anything else that will be needed in making the event a success. Your budget should take into account your fundraising goal, ensuring that you raise that resource above and beyond all expenses. Be sure to leave a little extra room in your budget for unforeseen costs.

4. Leadership:

As part of your fundraising efforts, your event would have a "host committee" and one or more "host committee chairmen." These figures are responsible for contributing reasonable amounts to the event and encouraging others to do likewise. The host committee is mostly composed of rich donors, business leaders, or local politically important personalities. The host committee and chairmen are not responsible for actually being in charge of the event, but are of utmost importance to ensuring you reach your fundraising goals. Your campaign should designate an event director and event staff / volunteers to organise the event.

5. Target Audience:

Who is the target audience for your event? Could this be a general fundraiser where everyone will be invited? Or is this event intended toward specific groups like business personalities, parents, or pro-lifers? Succinctly, you must decide whom you will invite to your event.

6. Set Up:

Your event staff should plan the event set-up well in advance. The set-up comprise all of the particulars of the actual event: Where will it be? Will food be served? Will there be entertainment? What sort of dress will be required? What is the proposed route for the event?

7. Marketing:

Just like a new good or service, your event needs to be aggressively marketed to your target audience. You need to convince your followers that your campaign and event are worthy of their time and resource. Draw up an entire marketing plan for the event. Plausible methods of "getting the word out" are: using the candidate's individual fundraising network, mailed invitations, direct mail, phone banks, word of mouth and the event host committee.

8. Sales:

Once you publicise your event, there must be steps in place for realising the actual ticket sales, or accepting donations for the event. You must decide whether there will be distinguished contribution levels for the event (such as a flat ticket charge, an extra charge to be invited to a V.I.P. reception in addition to the event, etc.). You must know who will sell the tickets, how they will be shipped or delivered, and who will be responsible for organising the incoming information.

9. Practice:

Whilstyou might not be needing a full run-through of your event, it is crucial that everyone who is working the event is aware, before time, what their duties are, where they should be during the event, and how the event is going to "flow." If you are having a large or a rather parallel event, the main event staff may want to have a practice run to make sure that your operation is running beautifully.

10. Thank-You:

Often times, the complaints from contributors to

political campaigns is, "They never even said 'thank-you.'" Ditto for campaign volunteers. Be certain your campaign takes the time to send thank-you notes to all who are involved in your event, including contributors, volunteers, staff and vendors. Keep your contributors ear, you're probably going to be expecting another donation sometime in the course of the campaign process.

Creating a Capital Campaign Plan

Capital campaigns can be difficult get around, time consuming endeavours for organisations of any size. No matter your nonprofit or campaign's budget, mission, or support level, taking on a long-term fundraising project on the scale of a capital campaign is simply complicated.

Yet, with a comprehensive capital campaign plan in place, your team be can rest assured that you'll be prepared to experience the challenges ahead and achieve your fundraising goals.

By working with the right political consultant, your organisation can develop a customised capital campaign scheme that outlines your route to flourish while addressing fundraising issues before they become a problem.

How to run a capital campaign successfully by outlining key steps in the planning period. Your campaign should:

1. Gather key players to help plan your capital campaign
2. Effect a capital campaign feasibility study
3. Set your capital campaign's budget
4. Develop fundraising collateral for your capital campaign
5. Inculcate a prospect list for your capital campaign

Are you set to know how to plan successful capital campaign? Let's set the ball rolling by breaking these steps down into some more detail.

1. Assemble necessary players to help plan your capital campaign

Apart from the profits in actually outlining your capital campaign from beginning to end, the capital campaign planning process can become an excellent grace to assemble the important players who will be critical to your campaign's success down the line.

Behind the scenes, it's critical that the responsibility of effecting your capital campaign isn't held by anyone or committee.

The postitive result of the campaign activities would not be of the candidate alone, but all other heads who had worked together. Also, your nonprofit can benefit during the planning process from the different perspectives that these individuals have to offer.

Let's go over some of the necessary roles that will come into play over the course of your capital campaign and how they fit into creating your capital campaign plan.

Capital campaign director

Every capital campaign should have a director leading the way from start to finish. This individual should singly focus on making the campaign a success and should be the guiding voice during the planning period.

Campaign consultant

Having a dedicated consultant to guide your nonprofit or campaign through the capital campaign process is crucial. When planning your capital campaign, a consultant can assist you to carefully pinpoint potential impediments and act beforehand to surmount them. Involve key insiders when forming your capital campaign plan.

The achievement of your capital campaign lies on your campaign's broad community of support working together and maintaining momentum during the several year span of your capital campaign.

By bringing important persons together during the planning period, your campaign not only benefits from their ways and areas of expertise, but also strengthens relationships between these individuals and your campaign

2. Conduct a capital campaign feasibility study

One of the central issues of how to start a capital campaign right is to conduct a feasibility study during the planning phase. A feasibility study assesses your campaign's readiness to take on the capital campaign before you begin.

Categorically, capital campaign feasibility studies are led by fundraising consultants. The positive default of this lies in the consultant's third-party perspective.

Since they are not dependents of the political campaign, they begin to work without internal political pressures watering their assessment of the capital campaign plan.

A central component of a feasibility study is interviewing staff, volunteers, donors, and other crucial players in the campaign to get a notion of their level as per support for the capital campaign plan.

As the consultant is a third party, interviewees are more likely to be honest than if a direct member of your campaign conducted the assessment. Your fundraising consultant can therefore experience from a more accurate dataset from which to determine the feasibility of your capital campaign.

Additionally, conducting interviews, your capital campaign's consultant will likely address some of the following areas of interest:

Case for support

Your capital campaign's case for support is what will gear passive supporters of your course into efficient donors. Over the course of the possibility study, your capital campaign consultant will decide whether or not your case for support is reasonable and compelling enough to contract donors.

Data integrity

The success of your capital campaign has to do with whether or not your donor data is dependable and informative. Are your prospect profiles imperfect or inaccurate? If the right data isn't in place, your consultant may posit channels to improve your data before the campaign starts.

Prospect relationships

It's this simple: without the proper prospect relationships in place, your capital campaign simply won't have the support it lacks to be a fundraising success. Your consultant will decide whether or not your campaign has built up enough prospect relationships that can be relied upon during the campaign and suggest how to improve cultivation where crucial.

Internal roles

A capital campaign consultant will also assess whether or not your team has the right people in the right roles internally. Should certain staff members have too much on their plate, not enough expertise in their areas of responsibility, or are otherwise unprepared for the job ahead, your consultant will suggest how to reform.

In addition to helping your team identify fundraising blindspots and upgrade your fundraising plan, your consultant will also be a key factor for your nonprofit throughout the capital campaign.

By establishing a relationship with a capital campaign consultant early on in the planning process, your campaign will benefit from having them on hand later in the campaign to aid in assisting to surmount any unforseen circumstances.

3. Set your capital campaign's budget

One of the most disregarded parts of successful capital campaign planning is budgeting for the necessary expenses related to carrying out your

Yes, You Can

fundraising plan.

Many campaigns make the mistake of thinking that austerity during budget planning will get them closer to achieving their fundraising goals eventually.

While this makes sense on the surface, the fact is that your campaign needs to invest in the necessary expertise and manpower to make your capital campaign work. If you fail to do so, your capital campaign will be disadvantaged from the beginning.

In partnership with your fundraising consultant, your campaign should set aside time during the capital campaign planning phase to set a perfect budget to cover the necessary costs associated with carrying out your fundraising scheme.

There are two main factors your nonprofit should put into consideration as you are setting your capital campaign's budget: the failure and achievements of your past fundraising plan budgets, and the budgets set by comparable campaigns

When it comes to identifying where past budgets have been functional proper, compare key expenses year over year with income associated with those areas. You might make a budget chart like the template below comparing previous expenses and income blending the same with anticipated expenses and income outlined by your preliminary budget.

Get to know the ways in actualising a capital campaign by mapping out your ideal budget using a budget chart.

After getting around the understanding of the feasibility of your capital campaign's budget based on past fundraising budgets, your fundraising consultant can go about the provision of insight into how your budget compares to those of comparable organisations which has semblance in campaigns.

As your consultant has experience working with other campaigns, this is another chance to benefit from their perspective as a third party. After making their assessment, they can predict and get you to acknowledge the situations where other political campaigns have approached setting successful capital campaign budgets.

Understanding how to run a capital campaign efficiently depends upon learning from your campaign's past fundraising successes and failures. Analyse past budgets carefully before making big financial decisions for your capital campaign.

4. Develop fundraising collateral for your capital campaign

Another crucial area of capital campaign planning is the collateral development process. Fundraising collateral could be referred to as the documents and resources, both private and public facing, that will be referred to throughout your capital campaign.

It is vital that these resources are entirely built on before the public phase of your capital campaign may start to be. Because these resources will be used internally by staff members and externally by prospects, it's integral that they are aligned in strategy and content.

As you continue to work with your capital campaign consultant, your political campaign will likely improve some of the following resources during the making of the phase of your campaign:

Case statement

In a capital campaign, political campaigns categorically develop a document called a case statement that is used to inform prospects of the campaign's fundraising needs; the case statement also appeals to supporters to contribute.

Prospect solicitation materials

These comprise of brochures, slide shows,

handouts, and other materials used when creating formal solicitations. These often are condensed versions of your case statement.

Fundraising website:

Adding to your campaigns's main website, your capital campaign itself should be running a section that you may refer prospects to for more information. The website should be equipped to accept online donations.

Gift range chart

Following, your feasibility study, work with your capital campaign consultant to revise your gift range chart. When effecting collateral, be sure to create a gift range chart resource to be referred to by both staff, volunteers, and prospects.

Your campaign may incorporate your gift range chart into a variety of collateral materials. For the public facing version of your gift range chart, be sure to brand it to your campaign and make it both attractive and easily understood.

Your campaign should develop capital campaign collateral with the knowledge of how it will be used behind the scenes and in front of prospects. Allow your fundraising consultant to help up your team on the right resources for your capital campaign.

5. Cultivate a prospect list for your capital campaign plan

In conclusion, one of the most important areas of your capital campaign's scheme which need addressing is how your campaign intends to cultivate and engage with prospects throughout the campaign.

To make your capital campaign a success, it's of utmost importance to ensure that you have identified the right prospects to provide the necessary gifts before your campaign can commence.

Showing lackadaisical attitude towards the existence of these prospects who are both capable and willing to give to your campaign, your team may lose to your fundraising goal.

In collaboration with your capital campaign consultant, you can determine areas of improvement by making enquiries on some of the following key questions:

Do we have an extensive list of identified prospects in line to approach for specific gifts on our gift range chart? Do we have backup prospects for every giving level?

If key prospects turn down our solicitations, do we have backup proposals ready to secure a smaller gift? Are there enough personnel in place to steward these prospects?

Do we have a major donor and planned giver possession strategy in place?

Further, one of the key markers of a successful capital campaign is a robust prospect pipeline. Throughout the campaign, your team should be laying the groundwork to gear up support for future political races by prospects you solicit.

The timeline of your future campaigns will be dramatically shortened if you already have a fund list of cultivated prospects on hand to turn to. During the planning process for this campaign, you may realise that you haven't done enough in the past to establish a prospect pipeline that would be worth relying on.

Working in conjunction with your campaign consultant, your team can identify areas of improvement in the prospect cultivation process. Once you've finalised your list of prospects, your consultant can device and help implement future best practices to ensure that your next campaign can benefit from thc the groundwork you've just laid.

If your political campaign wants to run a capital campaign successfully, it's vital to ensure that you have a comprehensive list of prospects in line before the campaign begins. Without reliable prospects on hand, you'll be trying to fundraise blindly.

When it comes to your campaign's next capital campaign, success lies in the designing process. With the right capital campaign plan in hand, your team will be equipped to tackle any challenge on the road in the course ahead. Good luck!

SECTION THREE
Surrounding Yourself with Winners

STEP TO SUCCESS FIVE

Find Your Political Partner

Campaign managers are duly responsible for the proper monitoring of the campaign strategy, including media relations and incorporating knowledge of demographics and election laws.

They are in charge of the candidate's calendar, plus deadlines associated with the campaign, events that would be beneficial to the candidate to attend and planned public appearances. Political campaign managers promote a candidate to win supporters, or in marketing, where they promote the sale of goods to the target markets.

Campaign Managers must be able to fulfil the following tasks in their job activities:

- Political campaign managers are the ones in charge of the rest of the team.
- They are responsible for all aspects of the research, drafting and execution of a statewide campaign scheme.
- They explain roles and negotiate contracts with all vendors, consultants, and staff including general, fundraising, field, and media.
- They hire and manage campaign staff.

- They lead the fundraising team by recognising and soliciting funds for a necessary fundraising campaign.
- They build broad, working grassroots campaigns including, but not limited to coalition building, voter registration, and networking
- They are able to oversee contact and get-out-the-vote activities.
- They oversee the growth of all paid media making, distribution and broadcast (TV, radio, and direct mail). Manage aggressive free media campaign.
- They staff statewide campaign committee and coordinate other statewide committees (for larger campaigns).
- They are in charge of all aspects of fiduciary oversight, legal administration and adherence to campaign finance reporting requirements.

Qualifications Expected

• Political campaign managers should have at least five years of political organising/campaign management experience, including experience with a statewide campaign where volunteer-executed voter identification played a central role.

• They must have a proven track record in coalition building, communities or field campaign coordinating, financial oversight, and public addressing.

• They must have knowledge in coordinating media purchase, making, and media relations.

• They must have fundraising exposure and knowledge of campaign funding sources.

• They must have the ability to work with diverse grassroots, serve as a team leader, and manage a sense with a sense of humor.

Traits of A tremendous Campaign Manager

Being a campaign manager shouldn't be taken for granted as a simple task. On the one hand, they have to deal with the candidate, who often knows less than the staff about the technical aspects of running a campaign but still prefers to overrule staff and consultant decisions. Then they also have to deal with the campaign staff, who are usually underpaid and overworked in the pressure-cooker environment of a political campaign, on the other hand.

Your campaign manager must:

1. Be a Politician

The candidate isn't the only person in a campaign who needs to be a politician. The campaign manager needs to possess the same skill set in order to run an effective and successful campaign. A thriving manager will need to massage numerous egos, from the candidate and his or her family to high-paid consultants, local volunteers, and major and minor donors. The agility to do so with grace and aplomb, and still being able to move the campaign in the direction they know it needs to go, is the real hallmark of a campaign pro.

2. Run the Campaign like a Business

Too many political campaigns falter as they are not run like businesses, and are instead treated like expensive hobbies or nebulous non-profits. The best campaigns are run in effect like corporations. Be watchful of the budget. Be decisive in smart cost / benefit decisions and track return on investment.

3. Focus on Systems

This tip goes hand in hand with tip #2 – Campaign managers have to be just that – managers. Professional business managers cannot engage in all the work, and don't expend all of their time on the technical aspects of their businesses. Instead they concentrate on setting up scalable systems that their staff can implement to bring success in a proven and effective manner. Unless the campaign they are managing is incredibly small, campaign managers should spend a good chunk of their time putting systems in place such as fundraising systems, grassroots systems, communications systems, etc. and managing their staff and volunteers in executing these methods.

4. Be a Political Entrepreneur

Entrepreneurs are minds who have a big vision, figure out a plan for getting there, and then execute that scheme. Plenty of people have big visions, but don't know how to get there. Other people can make plans but can't executive them. Entrepreneurs can do all three. Often, these skills are learned through practice and discipline. The best campaign managers in the business are true visionaries, they can cast a big vision for a campaign, write a scheme to get to that vision, and then manage the engraving of that plan.

5. Build up Your Own Base

Every campaign has various factions and loyalties. These groupings happen among the staff, the volunteer group, donors, the Finance Committee, and even the candidate's family. There are groups that will speak for one notion or tactic or another, who argue about message and strategy, who politely disagree on staff members and press release topics. As a campaign manager, you should be sure to calmly and intentionally mould up your own base of support.

You should do this not to direct or pose a threat to

your candidate or any other group, but so that when push comes to shove on an issue you have a group of supporters among the candidate's friends, donors, and consultants who will back your views. For instance, if you think the campaign message should be X, but the candidate's spouse thinks it should be Y, it's nice to have the relationships intact so that you can have a few key donors call the candidate to voice their support for your framing of the message.

Being a campaign manager isn't easy, it's a challenging and herculean position, no matter the size of the campaign. Go into the job armed with acknowledgement and a plan for winning.

STEP TO SUCCESS SIX

Building a Successful Team

Do you mean to form a successful work/political team? It can be hard and challenging as people bring everything about whom they are to a team. This includes, knowledge, values, past work experiences, upbringing, academics, prior team experiences, life and work goals, and skills in interaction and team building. But teamwork and conjunction can be taught and developed. You can use all of these tips and ideas to make a successful work team.

What Is a Team?

As humans, we spend our whole lives talking about teams. We begin on teams playing pee-wee soccer and baseball at four or five, and our team association never ends. Schools have sports teams, math teams, and debate teams. We pick tertiary institution and professional sports teams that we follow devotedly.

When you land in a job though, you are also on a team. Fundamentally, the meaning of a team is any group of people organised to work together principally and in unison to accomplish a purpose or goal.

Yes, You Can

You can participate in many diverse teams at work and you plausibly already do. But, your most basic team is usually your departmental team, the group with whom you are placed to make a product, a service, or even a campaign. Your end product either serves the company's external customers directly or the internal customers whom you support in making the product that does directly serve the customers.

How Do Business Teams Win?

A sports team wants to win, of course. A business/political team also wants to win, but its winning is not as clear-cut as that of a sports team. How does a team win? By accomplishing what the team has set out to accomplish.

Teams are created for both long term and short term communication. A product development team, an executive leadership team, and a departmental team are long lasting planning and operational groups. Their way of winning is to proceed to produce quality work and provide continued value to the firm.

They can realise success their value through strong sales (in the case of a sales team), or via reducing costs (such as an HR team that works to reduce turnover). Teams can also surmount when their new product (for a product development team) outperforms the competition. All similar to the

What Size Team Is Optimal for Work Performance?

The team size that is optimal for team performance is a topic much researched and debated. The plight is that you need to consider a number of factors when deciding optimum team size.

Factors that affect optimum team size include:

The reason for which you made the team, the anticipation you have of the team and its members, the course as per the team members need to play, the amount of cohesiveness and interconnectedness highly vital for astoundding team performance, and the function, activities, and goals of the team.

Therefore, optimum team size is not a sure answer. From experience and research, the optimum team size is 5-7 members.

It is much more likely that teams of a large size form sub-teams and active groups to accomplish the actual work of a project.

Larger groups are functional, as quinntessences, for strategic planning input, overall project communication, building support for an idea, and so forth.

Yes, You Can

As part of a political campaign team, there are many various roles that we must take account of:

Knowing Your Campaign Treasurer

Once upon a time in the world of elections and political campaigns, state election committees they only had to deal with one thin manual covering all state election rules. Local jurisdictions may have had structures in place, but these were casually enforced and perhaps casually obeyed.

The times of the volunteer bookkeeper / treasurer have ended.

Most committees now depend on their Treasurer for guidance, giving in to the ruling election law on day to day matters. Treasurers must be up to date on the rules pertaining to their committees, and the applications to several usual situations. For example, what are the disclosure requirements on a mass mailing? Can, a state PAC allow contributions in surplus of the calendar year limits? Can a membership association circulate a ballot measure petition to its membership without making an assistance to the ballot measure committee? Are living trust checks considered an individual or entity contribution under state law; under local law? And endlessly to infinity.

Today, the committee Treasurer is still in charge of establishing the local or state committee with the secretary of the state and federal committees with the Federal Election Commission. The Treasurer also manages the committee checkbook, reconciles the bank account and financial reporting software used for recordkeeping, accepts receipts for deposit and makes disbursements. Other duties have to do with recording loans, in-kind contributions and accrued spendings; providing financial updates to the committees as needed, gathering required contributor information and getting ready and filing required disclosure reports (filing electronically, as required). Additionally, the Treasurer normally responsible for the management of auditing files for the committee, consisting of the back up records demanded for all of the above pieces of business. Long after the campaign is over (and hastily forgotten or fondly recollected by the candidates, workers, consultants, fundraisers and/or sponsors) the Treasurer attends to audit complaints and sees the (sometimes long-closed) committee via the audit process.

Your Volunteer Coordinator

Volunteer organising duties have to do with recruitment, training, motivation, organisation, planning, and appreciation. This section will nudge you in the appropriate direction.

Training

Any polite volunteer recruitment strategy must include selling an outstanding or distinctive volunteer training program. Your volunteer organiser duties include the creation and promotion of that training program..

Motivation

Volunteer inspiration is arguably the most important of all of your volunteer coordinator duties. Again, asking for resource is herculean and it takes inspiration to be able to do it properly. It's an intense fear which can be overcome by enthusiasm. If your volunteers conceive in your benefits, then they will be without fictitious enthusiasm. This is the reason it is so important to make known your benefits often (varying it as much as is probable).

One way to make sure your volunteers are inspired during a specific campaign is to encourage them to support the campaign before they go out to ask the public to do the same. Let's take an example where your campaign is running a raffle and the volunteers are going to be out selling tickets amongst your community. Encourage your volunteers to get their tickets first before going out into the community. This makes selling much easier as the volunteers will actually feel less awkward about asking others to buy now they have already purchased. If you do this as part of your volunteer organiser duties, then you'll send out more staunch volunteers.

As a leader, your volunteer coordinator duties have to do with teaching your volunteers that as they are doing something unusual, its natural not to feel bold about it. The only way to build confidence is to start and try the manner of performance. When you began to ride a bike were you confident? What happened in twixt to make your habitude and confidence change? You tried, failed, tried failed, tried succeeded, tried and got better. You cannot build confidence without trying and failing, trying and succeeding. Use this to cheer up your volunteers before they go out to sell your candidate.

Your volunteer coordinator responsibilities have to do with getting volunteers to look at failure as a way to learn how to improve. Failure is how we learn and progress but somewhere along the line we learned that failure is a bad thing and you should take all necessary measures to avoid it. You must get away from that to begin to improve yourself.

Most people don't try anything as they are fearful of what the masses might say. Guess what, the people that would spew anything are as self-conscious as you. Let go what others think of you and do what you have to, in order to ace through.

Yes, You Can

If you succeed, great; if you fail, so what, you've acquired some knowledge about what doesn't work, file it and move on without pining (too long) regretting what had happened. The more you wait on things to happen, the more you fall behind. Start now. If your volunteers hear this message often enough they will start to get more comfortable with the concept of selling and they will be more inspired as a result.

Your volunteer organiser responsibilities also include looking after your volunteers. This assists them with inspiration. Praise them often and spend some resource on them, perhaps a lunch at Christmas. It'll be a small investment compared to what they can give in return. As a leader, you should make a point of praising them publicly at every opportunity, especially when they achieve their targets. Your newsletter, the local press and your website are great avenues where this can be achieved.

Give instances of what volunteers have achieved and the skills they have acquired. Thank all your fundraisers at your annual dinner dance and at your other events. The number one inspirer for any volunteer is your level of enthusiasm. When you're effecting your volunteer coordinator responsibilities, always do so with as much enthusiasm as you can. Let's say that again: the number one motivator for any volunteer is your level of enthusiasm.

Organisation

Volunteer organisation is another vital part of your volunteer coordinator duties. In terms of organisation the first thing you should do is ensure that you form a fundraising sub-committee that meets separately via the main committee.

The fundraising sub-committee has to do with nothing else other than fundraising activities. It's part of your volunteer coordinator duties to ensure that volunteers are focused on fundraising.

Not everyone who does fundraising for your organisation needs to sit on the fundraising sub-committee. Maybe in the early days when you have only four or five fundraisers it's meaningful for everyone to be on it, but when that number rises above 10, then I would keep the sub-committee down to 5 or 6. That said, I never turn anyone down if they show an interest in being on it.

Try to get a mix of people who are committed on the fundraising sub-committee in terms of, youth and experienced, male and female, optimistic and realistic. Try and select someone relatively new to be the leader of that group, rather than one of the more experienced people. Surely the more experienced people will be the main advisors but the idea is to get the newer heads to take more ownership and often you'll find they have newer, fresher ideosyncracies. Don't be fearful to take a chance on new and young people even if they fail as it's only through failure that you truly learn lasting lessons.

Give the group some targets and measure those separately from any other regular fundraising tussles you've got going. Utilise or establish connections with those targets to the funding of some of your organisations activities that won't allow funding from elsewhere (internally or externally), i.e. It stands or falls on their efforts. Allow the committee to run solely off other organisation activities, but ensure that it reports into the full committee at least once a month.

When you have founded a fundraising sub-committee that looks after the entire fundraising for your organisation, ascertain you continue to recruit new fundraisers anyway. What you can do then is set up a series of mini-projects for groups of new fundraisers, and then you appoint an experienced person to each group.

This gives the newcomers testing times that they perhaps would not get if they were to enjoin in your organisation's general fundraising populous. They may feel congested with too many experienced people around them; at least to begin with. You can as well try this with groups of young people, by way of introducing them to the liberty that come with being self-sufficient.

When you're setting targets for groups of fundraisers, be very clear about what you want them to achieve and put it into documentation. If appropriate, write down the milestones and track them because, sometimes the group might need a little push in the right direction. They must have the perception as if they are succeeding, and ideally it's better if they flourish on their own but it's better to give a required push than for them to feel purpose failure at any point.

When your volunteers are going out to sell your candidate to the public then sometimes it is good to allow an experienced volunteer with them so that they can percieve how to campaign (in easy and hard situations). It's one thing learning the theory but it's another putting it into practice. Sometimes, it's good to have them practice on each other beforehand in a few different situations (in their training). This may seem embarrassing to some volunteers but it's much less embarrassing than being faced with the same situation for real and not knowing what to do! The better prepared they are to deal with any situation, the more chance you have of them being a long-term volunteer.

Make sure that each person in the group is in charge of a specific set of tasks and responsibilities as they all need to feel as if they have contributed to the eventual success if they are to be glad in what they are doing. Make this part of their training in terms of teamwork training, i.e. If you are not fine with your involvement, never sit quietly and let your feelings fester, because subsequently, that doesn't help anyone.

Divide your volunteers in such a way that people know precisely who is covering what area and that you cover the entire community. Volunteer coordinator duties with respect to developing your organisational skills are a needed subject for you to master.

Planning

Planning is another big part of your volunteer conjunction responsibilities. You've heard the old cliché, "failing to plan is planning to fail." Well, guess what? It is absolutely true. You must plan what your objectives are for the campaign.

Poor planning is failing to fulfil your volunteer coordinator responsibilities as it means that you're not making best use of the limited time each volunteer has to give. This can have a very de-motivating result on the volunteers, which supremely has a stifling effect on organisational improvement. People perform better when they have clear direction and they can perceive (measurably) what they have attained.

When your schema is done, there's only three words for you: execute, track and measure. Execute the plan, track exactly what is happening on a weekly basis (make adjustments if crucial) and measure how your defaults match up with your plan.

Many people say to me, "what is the point of planning when it's always morphing as change they say is the most constant thing anyway." There's nothing bad with the plan changing when you have one to begin with (and there is a valid cause for the change). If you don't have a plan then yourcampaign will be mediocre in juxtaposition with what it could be. It's a big part of your volunteer coordinator responsibilities to assure ensuring your fundraising is maximised with proper planning.

Volunteer coordinator responsibilities also extend to best practices. There are some standard best practices that you have to integrate into your volunteers. The main one is: record everything. Record who got the tickets to sell, how many they got, how many they sold and the money they returned. I'm just using ticket selling as an instance, but anytime your volunteers do anything in fundraising, which involves handling resource, record it.

Yes, You Can

Full List of Key Members of Your Team

For many campaigns, most importantly smaller, down ballot campaigns, one person may hold many of these roles.

Additionally, many of these roles may be volunteers instead of paid employees. Regardless, once a role is assigned, the responsibility lies with that person.

Volunteer Coordinator

Volunteers in a campaign must be managed by someone very skilled. The Volunteer Coordinator ensures that volunteers are taken care of - well-fed, not over-worked and always busy. This post is sometimes shared among many staffers.

Canvass Director

A Canvass Director is solely responsible for developing, executing and overseeing a canvass strategy. The Canvass Director is responsible for managing their team of canvass leads and canvassers to implement the voter contact strategy to flourish. More so, Canvass Directors are responsible for ensuring that data is utilised adequately; including cutting walk lists, recording results, making proper survey questions, using advance targeting methods, etc.

Canvass Directors must have strong leadership

skills and the strength to manage a large staff. They are known for coaching canvass leads and canvassers to do their work effectively and holding them responsible to reporting their results daily. Applicants should have at least one cycle of field experience handling on a political campaign.

Campaign Manager

Campaign Managers are saddled with the responsibility of planning and organising a winning campaign and managing all aspects of the campaign organisation. Managers are also responsible for drafting and implementing a campaign plan and budget, hiring and managing a staff, overseeing fundraising and spending, and managing a candidate's priorities and schedule.

It's important for Managers to have strong leadership skills, prior experience in staff and budget management, and first hand experience overseeing polling, research, and paid media (such as mail or radio and television). Applicants should own a car and be prepared to relocate, and work long hours under pressure. Yes, applicants will need to have outstanding organisational and leadership skills.

Managers should have two to three cycles of political campaign experience.

Finance Director/Treasurer

The finance director handles the development and execution of the campaign fundraising plan. The Finance Director is also responsible for writing and implementing the campaign finance plan, then, managing the finance staff, and working hand in hand with the candidate, campaign manager and other campaign staff to ensure that finance goals are met. The Ideal finance director candidate will be extremely organised, have experience working with NGP software and will have a minimum of one cycle of strong finance experience as a finance director, finance assistant or call time manager.

Deputy Finance Director/Treasurer

Works with the finance director to successfully execute the finance plan. Responsibilities can include: Working with Finance Director to build and execute events, managing call time and tracking call results, drafting email and mail solicitations and staffing the candidate during events and meetings. Deputy Finance Director will be responsible for managing some finance staff and interns. Ideal candidate is organised and will have some campaign finance experience.

Call Time Manager

Works with the finance director to organise &

manage the candidate's fundraising calls. Responsibilities include: Preparing and tracking all calls; performing all call follow up; and managing and conducting all donor research. Ideal candidate is personable, organised and has some campaign experience.

Finance Assistant

Works with the Finance Director and Deputy Finance Director to successfully execute the finance plan. Responsibilities can include: conducting donor research, assisting with call time and tracking call results, processing contributions and expenses, NGP maintenance, providing assistance to the Finance Director and Deputy Finance Director with events by working with hosts to ensure goals are being met and other related activities. This is an entry level position, no fundraising experience is required, but any prior campaign experience is helpful.

Field Director

Field Directors are responsible for creating, implementing and executing a field plan in a large district. The Field Director is responsible for managing their team of field organisers to build the volunteer infrastructure necessary to execute the voter contact strategy to win. In addition, Field Directors are responsible for ensuring that data is utilised properly; including cutting walk lists, recording results, creating proper survey questions, using advance targeting methods, etc.

Field Directors must have strong leadership skills and the ability to manage a large staff. They are responsible for coaching organisers to do their work effectively and holding them accountable to reporting their results daily. Applicants should have at least one cycle of field experience working on a political campaign with staff management experience a must.

Field Organiser

Field organisers are keenly responsible for implementing and executing the field plan for their geographic region of your district. The field organiser is also responsible for the recruitment, training and management of a team of volunteers that will see to voter contact necessary to win. Also, field organisers are in charge recording results, all data entry for their area.

Field organisers are the heart and soul of any field program and must possess strong inter-personal skills and the ability to manage a team of volunteers for their discrete geographic area. They are responsible for training volunteers and coaching them to do their work effectively while also holding them accountable to reporting their results.

Communications/Press Director

Communication directors will work in tandem with campaign staff to formulate a comprehensive message platform for the respective electoral race and also see to the articulation and implementation of the candidate's manifesto and strategy through local and national media outlets as well as the print and electronic media for the electoral campaign. They are expected to be comfortable in interacting with members of the press. They are merely expected to be on the same wave length with other members of the campaign team. They are the image maker for the candidate and are expected to build an enabling atmosphere with members of the press.

Communications Directors are expected to be highly motivated and politically driven individuals. Priority consideration should be given to applicants with prior campaign experience and/or on the record experience. All applicants should have some background in communications and/or public relations linked to the political process.

Legal Advisor

It is also quite important to have a legal advisor as part of the campaign team. This legal advisor should be someone well versed in the machinations of the law especially the aspects that relate to electoral law and campaign finance.

Other Roles in Larger Campaigns

Field Staff:

- Policy Director
- Phone Bank Coordinator
- GOTV Coordinator
- Research Director
- New Media Director

Putting this all together and improving

Managers, organisation staff and Executives, and members universally explore ways to improve business results and profitability. Many view team-based, horizontal, organisation structures as the best design for involving all employees in creating business or even political campaign success.

No matter what you call your team-based improvement effort: continuous improvement, total quality, lean manufacturing or a self-directed work team, you are striving to improve results for the constituents in which you hope to govern.

However, few organisations are entirely pleased with the results their team improvement efforts yield.

If your team improvement efforts are not living up

to your expectations, this self-diagnosing checklist may tell you why. Successful team building that creates effective, focused work teams, requires attention to each of the following questions.

Clear Expectations

Has your leadership as the candidate concisely communicated the level of performance you expect of the team as well as the intended result to be delivered? Do members of the team have a clear understanding of the purpose of the team's creation?

Are you demonstrating constancy of purpose in supporting the team with resources of people, money and time? Does the work of the team receive sufficient emphasis as a priority in terms of time, attention, discussion, and interest directed its way by you?

Context

Obviously, you cannot board a train without knowing where it is headed. Does your team understand how the strategy of using teams will help you win your election?

Can team members outline the place of their team in the accomplishment of the common goals of the organisation? Does the team know how its activities fit into the larger context of the campaign's vision, goals, principles and values?

Commitment

Do team members show a high level of enthusiasm towards participating in the team's activities? What's the level of importance the team members give the team's mission? Are team members firmly committed to the overarching goal of accomplishing the team's mission?

Do team members recognise their input and contribution as being valuable to the campaign and to their own chosen positions? Do team members look forward to being recognised for their input to the team's operations? Do team members expect their skills to develop and grow in leaps and bounds on the team? Do team members have a feeling of excitement and challenge towards the opportunity afforded them by being on the team?

Competence

Do team members feel that there are seasoned experts on the team? (e.g., in a process movement, is each step of the process represented on the team?) Does the team feel that its members have the needed knowledge, skill, and capability to address the issues for which the team was created? If not, how well do the group have access to the help it requires?

Charter

Has the team painstakingly outlined and articulated its aims; its expected results and contributions; its timelines; and how it will measure both the outcomes of its work and the method the team employed to successfully finish their task? Does the leadership team or other coordinating group support what the team has designed?

Control

Is, the team, empowered with enough freedom to feel the ownership necessary to accomplish its set goals. At the same time, do team members perfectly understand their boundaries and limits? How far may members go in pursuit of solutions? Are limitations (i.e. monetary and time resources) defined at the beginning of the project before the team experiences barriers and rework?

Are the team's reporting accountability and relationship comprehended by all members of the campaign? Has the campaign defined the team's authority to implement its plan? To make recommendations? Is there a defined review process so that both the team and the organisation are persistently aligned in purpose and direction?

Do team members hold each other responsible for commitments, project timelines and outcomes?

Does the organisation have a plan to increase opportunities avenues for self-management among organisation members?

Collaboration

Do all team members understand the roles and responsibilities of team members? team leaders? Do team members have a clear understanding of group process? Do they know the stages of group development? Do team members effectively work together at interpersonal level?

Can the team approach goal setting problem solving, process improvement, and measurement collectively? Has the team established group rules or norms of conduct in areas such as, consensus decision making, conflict resolution and meeting management? Is the team utilising an appropriate strategy to accomplish its action plan?

Communication

Are team members clear about the relative importance of their duties? Is there an established means for members to give feedback and receive honest performance feedback? Is important business information provided regularly to the team by the candidate and campaign management team?

Is there a clear understanding of the entire context

for their existence? Is there a regular line of honest and transparent communication between team members? How often do team members bring novel ideas for consideration? When the situation arises, are necessary conflicts raised and addressed?

Creative Innovation

Does the campaign take keen interest in change? Does it in any way hold creative thinking in high esteem? Does it reward people who take sensible risks to make progress or does it simply reward the people who fit in and maintain the status quo ante? Does it create avenues for members to have access to books, educate and train its staffers?

Consequences

Do the team members have a sense of collective responsibility in terms of what they achieve as a unit? How often are rewards and recognitions given when teams attain successful heights? Are reasonable risks encouraged and respected in the campaign? Do team members point accusing fingers at each other instead of resolving problems?

Coordination

Are teams coordinated by a central leadership team that helps the groups to obtain what they need for success? Have priorities and resource allocation been planned across all departments?

Culture Change

Does the campaign recognise the salient fact that the team-based, collaborative, empowering, enabling organisational culture of the future is different than the traditional, hierarchical organisation it may currently be? Is the campaign planning to or in the process of changing how it recognises, rewards, appraises, hires, develops, motivates and manages the people it hires?

Does the campaign have a laid-down plan to utilise failures for learning and support sensible risk? Has the campaign discovered that the more it can transform its environment to support teams, the more it will get positive payback from the work of the teams?

Spend time and attention on each of these twelve tips to ensure your work teams contribute most effectively to your political success. Your team members will love you, your campaign will soar, and empowered people will "own" and be responsible for their work processes.

SECTION FOUR
Planning and Winning

STEP TO SUCCESS SEVEN

Make A Plan

Why plan your campaign?

Confidence in campaigning is indeed a product of being successful, but a good campaign plan is needed as well.

A good campaign plan needs to contain all of the following elements:

Campaign Aim

This is what you eventually want to achieve. It should be a short statement of what you want to do or what you wish to achieve.

Campaign Opportunities and Risks

This entails finding out what is happening on a particular issue at present, what has shaped the history of that particular issue and what could potentially happen in the near future. This could help you in unearthing an opportunity you could take advantage of to aid your campaign. Equally, you could discover potential issues that can derail your campaign or cause you difficulties.

This is imperative as it will help to shape your objectives, also the tasks you use to properly deliver the objectives.

Campaign Objectives

At this point, you break your campaign down into bite size units. These will enable you to achieve your overall campaign aim.

Campaign Stages

It is very unlikely that you'll be able to work on all your campaign objectives at the same time. A better way to do this is by looking at your objectives, what they respectively entail and the timeframe you've set for them to be achieved. It is only after this that you divide your campaign into different stages.

More often than not, your objectives will follow-on from each other in a logical sequence so that it will be quite clear in what order you should do things. But if not, look at the simple, easy ones to do, start with these and build up from there.

Campaign Tasks

For each stage, take the objective or part of the objective you are willing to work on, and break it down into the small tasks you will need to do to realise that. This will embrace things like conducting research, designing a leaflet, and designing a Get Out The Vote (GOTV) strategy.

The tasks should be as specific as possible, and should include details of how they are going to be done.

Campaign Action Plan

With the first stage of your campaign being worked out, and the major tasks needed to deliver that, you then need to put this information into an action plan. Draw a table with the objective (or part of the objective) you are going to be working on across the top, the different tasks listed under, then work out who is going to do each task, and when.

Try to have a column in your table for monitoring, so you are sure how you are going to check that you are on track. Probably the best way of doing this is to set aside 3-7 minutes at each meeting for reviewing your progress.

Campaign Contingency Plan:

There will continually be a chance for things to not go as planned. To be sure that this doesn't permanently derail your campaign, it is safer to be prepared with clear ideas of what scenarios could surface, and how you would handle/respond to these.

When planning your campaign, it's recommended you have the two things below:

Campaign Rationale

This should be a statement concerning why you are campaigning on this matter.

Why have you picked that campaign target, and why is it vital? This will guarantee you are all clear in your own positions about why you are going to run that specific campaign. This, in turn, will allow you to communicate convincingly with the public and media when they ask you about your campaign and the reason they should have an interest in it.

Campaign Message

This is a concise, snappy sentential remark that will be your critical communication tool with the public and media. It should be an unambiguous message about your campaign issue that you want your supporters to remember, and which will revitalise why the issue is essential and why people should care about it. It should be the pattern in which you engage people in your campaign.

Example Campaign Rationale

As an example: "This is the best time to be campaigning on recycling as the Council is under pressure to meet Government targets, and knows that in spite of having introduced a kerbside collection, without extra work to get more persons to use it, they are going to fail to meet their aims.

It's also a matter the local press have picked up on, so the Council do seem dedicated to doing something about it."

Example Campaign Message

"We need to extremely reduce our use of natural resources if we want there to be enough for future generations. Recycling is a perfect way to do this, as well as reduce the cost we bury in landfill sites which pollute the air, land and water.

You can help preserve the environment for your future generation simply by using your recycling bin."

Pre-campaign Plan

Successful campaigns demand outstanding planning. Let's do a walk though the key elements of a campaign plan.

A thoughtful, accurate plan will give your campaign its best shot at success. To assist you build your roadmap, let's review all the elements of an effective pre-campaign plan.

1. The Roadmap
2. The First 30%
3. Goals

4. Email Strategy
5. Team & Timing

Phase one: the roadmap

Prep for success with research and a clear plan

If you look at the fundraising from some of most fruitful campaigns, you'll notice politicians who met and surpassed their funding targets, are proven to be more successful in the long run. Behind every campaign is a thoughtful scheme for every stage of the project. Most successful politicians are typically intentional with every aspect of their timing.

Phasae two: the first 30%

Launch your campaign with your first 30% funding already in place

After aiding dozens of political campaigns, 30% is a significant number to recollect. Campaigns that scale up 30% of their targets in the first stretch of their campaigns are substatially more expected win in the long run. By racing quickly to 30%, you build important early momentum and give prospective backers confidence that your campaign is on track, the mother aim of a campaign.

Phase three: goals

Set attainable goals and think in stages

Setting your goal can be the hardest part of starting a campaign, and there are diverse strategies to evaluate, including funding your project in stages. Most campaigners that raise millions of dollars begin by launching a smaller, more managable, campaign, and started to increment their audience from there.

Other campaigns have experienced success by setting a low to moderate goal, which can help build confidence with backers early in the campaign. If you want to raise $20,000, for example, consider instead aiming for $15,000 and making $20,000 your stretch goal. Most political campaigns utilise a combination of these techniques to get to their ultimate goal.

Phase four: email strategy

Never undervalue the power of email to excite and rally your constituents. Research indicates that the average conversion rate from email is 34% higher than on any other forms of outreach, making it an ideal method for engaging followers. Compared with social media posts or public relations efforts, email helps you to quantify how many potential supporters were reached with your information and how many responded, letting you know precisely if your engagement efforts have yielded a return. There are a number of free email tools like *MailChimp* and *Gmail* that you can use to begin your email outreach.

Phase five: team and timing

Build a team to divide and conquer on tasks

Make no mistake a political campaign can demand a lot of ongoing work, maybe even on par with a full-time job. Ascertain you have enough people-power available to make the best of the experience. Whether you're working with professional political operatives or simply family and friends, a well-organised team can help amplify your message by posting to social media, responding to enquiries or updating your campaign page. In addition, work closely with your team to set aside ample time in the planning stages. As a general rule, reserve at least 60 days to set a structure for the campaign and 30 days to review, and maintain it after launch. With a campaign team readied, you'll be able to make and manage more in those 90 days than you could alone.

STEP TO SUCCESS EIGHT

Get Out There!

Your "Get-Out-The-Vote" (GOTV) messaging may be one of the most valuable and necessary components of your entire political campaign.

Why? Get-Out-The-Vote efforts not only derive greater support and get people enthused about a campaign, but it also directly reflects your backup of the important American right to democracy.

The key with Get-Out-The-Vote campaigns is that voters must be targeted – that is, it's critical to ensure that you are getting your followers, not your rival's, to go to the polls. At the end of the day, Get-Out-The-Vote operations are a waste of valuable time if you are trying to move all voters to the polls, including your opponents'.

No matter what your campaign budget, or plan is leading up to the election, it is crucial that every campaign carefully plans and executes a Get-Out-The-Vote strategy. Simply put, whether you are campaigning for City Council or for President of the United States, every campaign should execute this strategy.

Where to get started.

A campaign's Get-Out-The-Vote should begin well in advance of Election Day. Throughout the campaign, staff and volunteers should be gathering names and information of voters in your district who plan to vote or have historically voted. Significantly, campaigns should have their Get-Out-The-Vote team in place about six months prior to the first votes being cast. The team should come up with a detailed plan featuring stratagies it will utilise to reach these voters, as well as a budget for these activities.

There are a number of ways to collect names. Your campaign should always gather this information – typically name, address, phone number and email – during all of its activities, including events and fundraisers.

Your campaign should also differentiate which voters are ready to vote for you during candidate door-to-door campaigning. This should comprise developing strategies that will send canvassers house-to-house with campaign materials to discuss the upcoming election with potential voters. This gives voters an opportunity to make enquiries, become engaged and read over materials about the campaign. Most importantly, it can assist your team member's ability to track each and every voter contact and relay information back to the campaign.

The Final Countdown

The key to get-out-the-vote efforts is interaction. A campaign's goal should be to ascertain that each and every voter who has been identified actually votes.

Pending on the campaign budget, you should start ramping up your GOTV campaign a few weeks to a few months before to the first votes being cast. At this juncture, team members should be contacting each voter who has been made known as a supporter, encouraging them to go out and fulfil their constitutional rights. Each supporter should be informed on multiple occasions through diverse or various mediums.

There are several ways you can contact these supporters – a phone bank that calls each supporter to remind them to go vote; digital or hard copy literature drops and door-to-door visitations; and, direct mail messages which would reinforce your message. The best option is to incorporate a wide variety of these approaches to to get to each supporter multiple times.

Today, Get-Out-The-Vote is so much more than a political buzzword – it's a crucial component of victory for political candidates. And in a close election, it can mean the distinguishing line between victory and defeat.

You should activate get-out-the-vote tactics into any political campaign, large or small. From rallies and family-friend events to word-of-mouth marketing, be creative when it comes to the grassroots struggles you take on, taking great pains to ensure that every effort is in line with your campaign's overall messaging.

Making the best Use of GOTV

Every campaign, no matter how small, should have a scheme in place to make Get-Out-The-Vote calls in the days leading up to Election Day. Ideally, your campaign will have kept a list of followers over the course of the campaign, drawing on all of your campaign activities to grow and cultivate that list.

If your campaign has built such a list, then this is the list that will be the basic building blocks of your phone operation. Preferably, each person on this list will have at least one phone call from your campaign, in addition to any other Get-Out-The-Vote activities your campaign conducts. Of course, many campaigns reach the final weeks of the election cycle and realise that they need to make calls but haven't created such a list. Don't get caught with your trousers down! Be prepared!

GOTV calls are so important that you still need to

do them, even if you haven't had a formal list of staunch followers. The key to effective GOTV calls, and Get-Out-The-Vote activities in general, is pinpointing who is likely to back you up and motivating them to go to the polls.

The first step in building any Get-Out-The-Vote list is compiling the names and phone numbers of all of the candidate's friends and family who are registered to vote in the district in which the campaign is being waged. Add to that list all of the volunteers and donors to the campaign who live in the district and are registered to vote. Prompt your volunteers to list any friends or family who they know support the candidate and are signed up to vote in the district. For the campaign that begin early, this is just the starting of the GOTV list. For the campaign starting just days before the election, this list may be your entire get-out-the-vote call list.

The Time to Call

Your GOTV call operation should begin as early as it takes to land a call to every person on your list, but not so early that the persons you call will forget you called. Recollect – our goal is to know the people on that list to go to the polls. For that purpose, the closer to Election Day you make your calls the better.

A good rule of thumb is to try to begin making

calls no earlier than the Tuesday before the election (Thursday is assumed better) and to end your calls on Monday night, the day before the polls open. Always remember not to call too early or too late. Early-late evening works best. If no one is home, leave a message on the answering machine and count it as a "completed call." If no one is home and there is no answering machine, try and note that number to be re-called later.

Setting Up Shop

If you've made a sizeable call list, consider finding some volunteers to help you make your calls. Be sure to train them properly. Make them viable sales representatives prompting them with a a script for making the calls, goals for achieving the required amount of calls, etc. Preferably, your volunteers will be able to work out of your campaign headquarters so that you can personally supervise their activities. If this is not possible, then have them make the calls from their own homes. In this case, training is quite vital.

Communication

Your GOTV phone calls can be succinct and to the point. Remember, you don't need to get information from the person being called, and no need for persuasion from you, they are already supporters or probable supporters. You simply need to remind them of the candidate's name and remind them to vote for the candidate on Election Day. Here's a simple script or message your volunteers can use:

"Hi, this is John calling on behalf of the Michael Burns for Congress Campaign. Election Day is this Tuesday, and the polls are open from 7am until 7pm. Please remember to vote for Michael Burns for Congress this Tuesday."

So brief and on point – Say the candidate's name and the office he or she is running for at least twice, tell them when the election is, and move on to the next call.

Why GOTV Campaigning?

There is a conscience plan behind a booming Get-Out-The-Vote campaign—and it works.

Post-victory, it is vital to look back at what worked and how it can be enhanced upon in the upcoming elections in the next few years. Additionally, people get indolent when their Party is already in office so GOTV in mid-terms—where you already hold the majority—is actually more vital. Campaign managers and staffers know it is never too early to start thinking about GOTV for the next election cycle so let's talk about the importance of having a strategy that is effective.

- **Social Wins.**

Now that everything we do can be stored online and disseminated to friends, the social pressure—and encouragement—to vote may be the most important factor in GOTV. As social networking and online applications improve, there will always be ways to integrate GOTV plan in more powerful, personal, and effective ways. Stay ahead of the curve on the technology behind social reach advertising to ensure this top priority gets the attention it merits.

- **The Registration Factor.**

Registering to vote is simple, but it is yet one of those "annoying" things people have to monitor. Do not leave the duties of finding a place to register up to the slackers. Select your demographics and show up where they dwell, work, eat, play, and sleep. Snatch them up and even the irritated will be likely to take 30 seconds to register. There are certain places to appear so do some research and camp out where you will get the most bang for your buck.

- **Keeping in Constant Contact.**

As soon as voter registration is in full swing, start effecting the use of new voter lists available to you. Grabbing and utilising new voters when they first register is imperative in creating a new relationship with long-term potential. You want to create a positive impression right off the bat, while new voters are still patting themselves on the back for doing their civic duty to register. Continue impressing at public places where voters hang out, showcase your message in spontaneous ways which works for certain demographics, and cultivate experiences that will be part of their lives after they leave your presence.

- **GOTV Volunteers.**

There are members of your campaign staff and there are regular personalities you can instigate positively to help you as campaign volunteers. These folks never had it in mind to be involved but you reel them in with opportunities like:

Happy hour

Pizza parties

Free t-shirts, stickers, pens, etc.

Perks for friends and family

Focus group participation with candidate

Personal appreciations from the candidate at speeches and events-

- **Online Volunteers.**

Different from traditional GOTV volunteers,

online volunteers are persons of affluence you specifically recruit to work with you throughout the campaign. Writers, bloggers, and Twitter and Instagram influencers have large mouthpieces and few gatekeepers. Create a specific plan to feed them helpful stories, easy and interesting coverage, exclusive interviews, photos, and more. Give these content creators a reason to be on your side. They want to get traffic and buzz, and so do you. Work collectively with like-minded people to cultivate a GOTV effort like none other.

- **Verbal Commitment.**

You need a solid GOTV canvassing team that can use your campaign's well-integrated walk book to scour the most crucial neighborhoods and get people committed to voting for you come Election Day. Getting a verbal acknowledgment from voters concerning when they plan to show up to vote will assist in cementing their commitment in their minds. Assume you will be hanging out at the polling station most of the day and ask your potential voter this: "What time will I see you at the station on Tuesday?" Research establishes act on a particular plan, in which they are more likely to follow through.

- **Merging Offline and Online.**

The widest experience a potential voter can have will happen when their online and offline experiences merge. Signing up to vote offline, then seeing that experience get to them online via email or advertising right afterwards will secure that will to vote. Additionally, persistently interacting with potential voters online through email and advertising will set them up to join you offline at an organised event. When the online and offline worlds meet, a strong bond is established. That is why it is so vital to recognise the power of social media. Making a campaign hashtag to use at events or executing real-time Twitter conversation in the room will make your candidate seem like a more integral part of someone's life. They will, therefore, feel more indebted to take time out of their busy day to vote.

• **Well-Executed Events.**

Organising a positive event for your candidate in a popular, simple access location, will work miracles for your GOTV efforts. Be politically inclined about where to hold the event—where are the voters you actually want to hit? Meet them in reality. Be certain you get the optimal time, place and date, as well as knowing which matters to focus on. An inspiring campaign speech may make one have a change of heart voting for you or not in a quick second. Ensure the direct and indirect time to time usage of the social media by having people around "check in" on Facebook when they arrive, launch a pre-populated tweet with hashtag, have a social media photo booth and social media kits to bring home with them to use. Fill the event schedule with interesting, short bursts and do not let anyone depart without giving them encouragement to see them on Election Day at the polls!

These are just a few ways you can prioritise your GOTV struggle in the upcoming election cycle. Even the best candidate in the world will not win if they do not put into consideration a winning campaign team supporting them getting out the vote at sensitive times.

The power and effectiveness of social network in GOTV will aid or break a campaign these days, so take these powerful ideas to heart and design ways you will use them. Time is everything and guess what? It's already counting down.

IN CONCLUSION

All of these tips and tricks of the trade will never make up for the passion and dedication that you and your team pour into your campaign, but they can lead you in the right direction. Running for election and standing for what you and your constituents believe in is a noble thing, never forget that. Never forget that YOU are a representative of others and not of yourself. Use this guide to not only win your campaign, but set yourself up to do some good once elected.

Now that you've armed yourself with this guidebook, get out there, make a difference, and win your election!

Printed in Great Britain
by Amazon